LET KIDS BE KIDS

LET KIDS BE KIDS

Rescuing Childhood

Dr. Mary E Muscari

SCRANTON: University of Scranton Press

Library of Congress Cataloging-in-Publication Data

Muscari, Mary E.
  Rescuing childhood : let kids be kids! / Mary E. Muscari.
    p. cm.
  Includes bibliographical references and index.
  ISBN 1-58966-118-4
  1. Children–Social conditions. 2. Child psychology. 3. Parent
  and child. 4. Child welfare. 5. Children's rights. I. Title.

HQ767.9.M87 2006
 305.231–dc22

                                                    2006042094

Distribution:

**The University of Scranton Press
Chicago Distribution Center
11030 South Langley
Chicago IL 60628**

PRINTED IN THE UNITED STATES OF AMERICA

DEDICATION

This book is dedicated to my parents, Joseph and Mary Muscari, whose advice I still seek, even though it's now only in my prayers. And to my "children," who patiently waited by my side to see this book finished: Mystique, Chelsea, Sabrina, Effie, Shelby, Arielle, Mona, Zoe, Travis, Bubba, Dakota, Gus, Missy, Brandy, Gizmo, Kai-lee and Parker.

CONTENTS

ACKNOWLEDGMENTS

The author wishes to thank the following people for their help in making this project a reality:

Jeffrey L. Gainey
Director, University of Scranton Press

Patricia A. Mecadon
Production Manager, University of Scranton Press

Fr. Richard W. Rousseau, S.J.
Former Director, University of Scranton Press

Grapevine Design,
For the cover design

John Hunckler,
Copyeditor

The author of the section "Plants to Pets" in Chapter 10:
Jack S. C. Fong, MD, CM, MSc, FRCP (C)
Chairman, Department of Pediatrics
Danbury Hospital, Danbury, CT
Associate Clinical Professor of Pediatrics
Yale University School of Medicine, New Haven, CT

The author also wishes to thank the following faculty and staff from the University of Scranton for their photo contributions:

Satya P. Chattopadhyay, BME, PGDM, PhD
Associate Professor
Management Marketing

Carolyn F. Matrone
Program Coordinator
Continuing Education

Cheryl Phillips
Sr. Administrator Information Tech Events

Patricia A. Mecadon
Production Manager, University of Scranton Press

The author also wishes to thank Trinka Pettinato, cover designer, for her photo contributions.

Ongoing Consultants:

Christopher Daniel Muscari
Age 10
Attends Alden Place Elementary School
Loves sports, math, and attending school

Gianna Maria Muscari
Age 8
Attends Alden Place Elementary School
Loves softball, cheerleading, soccer, and swimming

Daniella Susanna Muscari
Age 4
Loves animals, reading stories, listening to stories, and reading books

INTRODUCTION

In 1999 when I first set out to find ways to help parents raise nonviolent children, I had no idea where that journey would eventually take me. My initial research resulted in my writing *Not My Kid: 21 Steps to Raising a Nonviolent Child*, a book that focused on the factors that tend to make some kids more violent and those that can help make other kids more resilient. But that research turned out to be only my first steps along a road of discovery.

As I toured to country, speaking to parents and professionals alike, I was asked about how to keep kids from becoming violent, and also about how to keep kids safe from violence—safe from the unspeakable: abductors, molesters, Internet predators and terrorists. These latter concerns let me to research and write *Not My Kid 2: Protecting Your Children from the 21 Threats of the 21st Century*, which also included threats such as stress, the media, negative peers, and drugs. Eventually, this line of inquiry led me to examine the question that today's parents and professionals ponder on a regular basis:

How can we protect *and enrich* the lives of children today?

Exposed to profanity, violence, and sex—both real and virtual—many of today's children are prevented from enjoying their childhood, a problem that is both a cause and an effect of the millennium's growing dangers. For many, this is compounded by an unrelenting push and a frenzied pace throughout childhood.

In the US, we commonly believe that each generation of children should enjoy better lives than their parents did. But today's kids are fatter, more frazzled, and exhibit more signs of mental illness. Many times, we see a protected and enriched childhood being edged out in favor of a sort of premature adulthood—pushing aside joy and wonderment in favor of pressure, rigidity, and anxiety. Many of our children encounter the temptations and threats of alcohol and drugs, while marinating in a culture that undermines community values and responsible behavior. Far too many of them are oversexualized, foulmouthed, or aggressive. Others are overscheduled and overstressed. Too many don't know how to play without adult instruction or licensed toys. Lacking protection and enrichment, children can grow to be incomplete adults who might never fully understand what it is they're lacking.

We all see it happening, and we all want to do something about it. But the keys to protecting and enriching our children's lives are not readily available in one place. So I decided to add a third volume to my child-rearing series. Taking the same approach that I used for the first two *Not My Kid* books, I dove into research, experience and expert opinion to examine variables that affect childhood and to gather and present user-friendly ways to let kids be kids.

Each chapter tackles challenges faced by adults with children today: finding time for love and attention, growing as a family, keeping healthy, and staying safe. Some chapters focus on areas of childhood so often crowded out they can be forgotten—citizenship, spirituality, creativity and unstructured play. Others center on helping children experience their uniqueness, find their true heroes, and get back to nature. Finally, there are chapters on assisting kids to make a joyful noise, and retain their youthful innocence. All provide step-by-step, easy to read answers for today's time-crunched and perplexed parents.

Childhood is the foundation of adulthood and in retrospect can be a glorious reminder of what is right in the world. If we continue to allow the degradation of positive childhood experiences, what will future generations of children be like? Imagine the joyful squeals of children playing in tree-filled parks replaced by vulgar voices echoing near empty asphalt playgrounds. Imagine humankind without silliness, awe, imagination, inspiration and resourcefulness. As we act to protect and enrich the lives of our children today, we ensure against such a tomorrow.

Please join in this critical effort to protect and enrich the lives of children and let kids be kids.

Part One
Survival Needs

1

LOVE AND ATTENTION

Studies show that when children receive consistent love and attention from early infancy onward, it positively affects their social, physical, mental, and emotional development. Their ongoing need for love and attention is as essential as their need for food, shelter, and clothing. When we, the responsible adults, help to provide today's children with consistent love and attention, we sow the seeds of better lives for them and a better world for all of us.

*****

Children feel important when parents pay attention to them and show interest in their activities and efforts. It's sometimes easy to forget to pay attention to children when faced with a multitude of demands on parental time, including household chores, work, civic duties, and social activities. But children need attention, and they try hard to get it, even if that means being disruptive or obnoxious. When children feel rejected or unappreciated, they often resort to misbehavior which, unfortunately, can lead to further rejection and less attention, creating a vicious cycle.

In order for children to learn to respect and care for others, they need parents to provide a loving, warm, caring, and respectful environment for them. All humans need love, and children are no exception. They need the unconditional love of their parents if they are to develop into happy, well-adjusted adults. Studies show that children who know they are loved will most likely turn out well, have high self-esteem, achieve at a higher academic level, and have healthier relationships. Children who are deprived of love are more likely to have low opinions of themselves and others, tend to be lower academic achievers, and may be more inclined to join a gang, become entangled in the legal system, become parents too soon, and/or suffer from a greater number of physical and emotional problems.

ATTACHMENT

We form hundreds of relationships throughout life. Some are enduring and intimate. Others are transient and superficial. Together, all relationships form the glue of family, community, and society. The ability to form and maintain relationships is a very important trait of humankind, because without it we would not learn, work, procreate, or survive very well. The earliest and most critical of all relationships are attachment bonds, which are initially created through an infant's interactions with parents or with other primary caregivers. These first relationships help define our capacity for attachment and set the tone for all of our future relationships.

Coined by John Bowlby in 1958, *attachment* refers to the selective emotional ties that an infant or child demonstrates for another person or persons, for a pet, or even for an object (e.g. security blanket). Infants form attachments to their caregivers, usually their parents, during a focused relationship that develops over time through repeated contacts and attachment behaviors—visual tracking, grasping, reaching, smiling, babbling, clinging, and crying.

Attachment gives children a security base, which at first provides a source of strength and identity, and later supplies a point of differentiation and separation. Most babies form multiple attachments. These attachments are similar in quality, but differ in intensity and are not freely interchangeable. When stressed, an infant seeks comfort and security first from the person nearest the top of her attachment hierarchy.

In order to have a secure base from which to explore the world, handle stress, and form meaningful relationships, every infant needs a primary adult who cares for her in sensitive ways and who perceives, makes sense of, and responds to her needs. Mothers usually act as primary caregivers. However, fathers, other relatives, or non-relatives can function as primary caregivers if they sustain a central role in the child's life for at least the first three, and preferably for five years—the period of time when a child's brain develops most rapidly.

Dr. Ainsworth described two types of attachment—*secure* and *insecure*. She further divided insecure attachment into *avoidant* and *resistant* attachment.

SECURE ATTACHMENT

Patterns of secure attachment develop when the caregiver shows sensitivity to the infant's signals, acceptance of the infant's distress, and a consistently positive parenting style. The caregiver seems to align her own internal state with that of her child and communicates this alignment in nonverbal ways that the child understands. This forms a bond of trust, love, and respect that the child feels and responds to.

Most infants demonstrate secure patterns of attachment. This is considered optimal. A securely attached infant freely explores her world in the presence of her caregiver, checks on her caregiver periodically, and restricts exploration in the caregiver's absence. She shows distress in the caregiver's absence and responds positively to the caregiver's return. She seeks out the caregiver when upset and settles down when comforted.

INSECURE ATTACHMENT

Generally speaking, insecure attachment results when a parent or caregiver is less responsive to a child's distress signals. The adult becomes unavailable physically, psychologically or emotionally and tends to be insensitive or unpredictable in response to the attachment needs of the infant.

Avoidant attachment   The caregiver of a child that develops avoidant attachment behaviors does not provide adequate comfort when the child becomes ill, hurt, or upset. The child learns he cannot rely on the caregiver to meet his physical and emotional needs. Avoidant children limit their emotional expression (possibly to avoid experiencing further rejection).

An avoidantly attached child seems unconcerned as to whether his parent is absent or not. He explores his environment without interest in his parent's whereabouts, and reacts with minimal distress when his parent departs. When the parent returns, an avoidant child does not move toward the parent or initiate contact; he actually ignores or avoids the parent. Despite the apparent lack of concern, an avoidant child shows as much or more physical arousal, suggesting that he has learned to contain his distress.

Resistant attachment   The Parent or caregiver of a child that develops resistant attachment behaviors tends to be inconsistent when responding to the child's distress signals. So the child devotes a lot of energy to eliciting the caregiver's aid.

The child shows exaggerated expressions of attachment needs. She hesitates to explore her environment, and seems preoccupied with getting the caregiver's attention. She becomes extremely upset when the caregiver leaves. When the caregiver returns, the child will either seek or resist contact. When she does seek contact, she has trouble settling down and responds poorly to her caregiver's attempts at soothing her.

Disorganized/disoriented attachment   Another researcher, Mary Main, added a fourth category (disorganized/disoriented attachment) to describe the attachment behaviors of children who do not easily fit into Ainsworth's original categories. Many of these children have been abused or have parents who suffered severe trauma. They have been subjected to highly stressful, chaotic, and frightening environments. Even short-term stress such as moving, or the birth of a sibling, can temporarily cause a disorganized pattern of attachment.

These children either lack organization in their patterns of behavior or have strategies that repeatedly break down. When stressed, these children appear disorganized or disoriented, behaviors that may be interpreted as fear or confusion with respect to their caregivers. These behaviors include approaching the caregiver with head averted, freezing trance-like, or exhibiting strange postures.

FACTORS THAT AFFECT ATTACHMENT

Caregiver behavior strongly affects the development of attachment. And several factors influence caregiver behavior. Nurturing feelings don't always accompany biological motherhood, and various factors affect maternal behavior with a newborn. Some that resist change include the woman's level of maturity, how she was reared, cultural variables, relationships with her family and partner, experiences with previous pregnancies, and financial worries. New mothers need emotional support, especially when they return home within twenty-four hours of delivery. They're often exhausted, sore, and may be overwhelmed with emotion and responsibility.

Nurturing feelings don't always accompany biological fatherhood. Factors that affect paternal behavior include level of education, participation in prenatal classes, role concept, the sex of the infant, attendance at delivery, early contact, and the feeding method of the baby. Emotional support from the mother can reduce stress levels for the father. This might be because men maintain intimacy and self-disclosure primarily in their partner relationship.

Since attachment is a two-way process, infant factors play a role. Some babies are better than others at eliciting good caregiving. These infants are usually happy and easy to care for. They smile when played with, eat and sleep at regular times, and are good at teaching adults how to be good parents. When cared for competently, they're quick with a smile.

ATTACHMENT ACROSS THE LIFESPAN

Children need to feel they are loved and cared for. Utilizing the results of research studies that compared the quality of mother-child attachment during the first two years of life with later outcomes, Dr. William Sears developed a list that shows how securely attached and insecurely attached children differ in several areas.

- Behaviors as infants and toddlers
  - Securely attached children tend to be secure, trusting, and interdependent, and they learn early how people treat each other.
  - Insecurely attached children tend to be clingy, anxious, distant, angry, dependent, disorganized, and impulsive.

- Obedience
  - Securely attached children tend to be open to redirection, they expect to behave, and want to please.
  - Insecurely attached children tend to protest against redirection; feeling controlled, they can be oppositional and devious; at times they don't seem to know what behavior is expected.

- Getting along with friends
  - Securely attached children tend to be sociable, considerate, cooperative, popular and willing to share; they mix well with all age groups and have deep lasting friendships.
  - Insecurely attached children tend to be aggressive, manipulative, and unwilling to share, they can become bullies or victims—isolated, distrusting, and unpopular, having shallow friendships.

- Preschool behaviors
  - Securely attached children tend to be curious and eager to learn; they can be social leaders.
  - Insecurely attached children tend to be hesitant and less curious to learn.

- Empathy and caring
  - Securely attached children tend to be sensitive and are willing to help their friends.
  - Insecurely attached children tend to be selfish and unsympathetic.

- Problem-solving ability
  - Securely attached children tend to be enthusiastic, persistent, less frustrated, responsive to instruction, an adaptable.
  - Insecurely attached children tend to be negative, easily frustrated, and less adaptable; they are likely to give up quickly.

- Self-worth and confidence
  - Securely attached children tend to have self-confidence based on realistic self-appraisal.
  - Insecurely attached children tend to lack self-confidence.

- Show of emotions
  - Securely attached children tend to be appropriately expressive and affectionate.
  - Insecurely attached children tend to hold in feelings, display uncontrollable anger, and have inappropriate zreactions.

- Use of adult resources
  - Securely attached children tend to expect help and use facilitators wisely; they tend to be confident in conversations with adults.
  - Insecurely attached children tend to be distrustful; they avoid eye contact and do not seek help.

- Sense of right and wrong
  - Securely attached children, when wrong, show signs of having healthy guilt stemming from a developed sense of right and wrong.
  - Insecurely attached children have a confused sense of right and wrong, and tend to show no remorse.

- Adult outcome (how they grow up)
  - Securely attached children tend to grow up to be morally mature, are more likely to have fulfilled relationships, are less prone to addictive habits, and are more psychologically stable.
  - Insecurely attached children tend to grow up to be morally immature; they have a higher risk of violent and sociopathic behaviors, addictive behaviors, and problems with intimacy; they are less likely to have fulfilling relationships.

Evidence indicates that attachment affects people's well-being in profound and enduring ways across the lifespan. In general, secure attachment appears to act as a protective factor against emotional and behavioral problems during childhood and adolescence. Children who are securely attached at age one tend to be resilient, resourceful, cooperative, and popular with peers in preschool. Avoidantly attached children can become emotionally isolated, hostile, or antisocial during the preschool or school years, especially in the presence of other risk factors, while resistantly attached children tend to be dependent, easily frustrated, and attention-seeking.

Children exhibiting disorganized/disoriented attachment behaviors have the greatest risk for developing aggression, conduct disorders, and dissociative disorders (mental illnesses that involve disruptions or breakdowns of memory, awareness, identity, and/or perception) later in life.

MAKING TIME FOR YOUR CHILD

Your child wants and needs your time. Spending time together is a prerequisite of protecting and enriching her life by showing her love and attention. Your child comes to learn what you value by observing how you spend your time, and she learns that she is loved and valued when you give her what matters most—your time, love, and attention.

But with so many demands on your time, it's often difficult just getting together for a family meal, let alone spending additional *quality* time with your children. First, commend yourself for what you're already doing with your children. Then realize you can't create any more time than you have, but you can learn to reallocate it in order to make the most of it.

The Nebraska Cooperative Extension suggests you make better use of your time by dividing it into seven categories:

1. Family time: Separate your activities. Leave work at work, so you can concentrate on yourself and your family once you are home. Have a family meeting once a week to coordinate calendars and plan events and activities. Set up "family fun time" once a week, and set up weekly *one-on-one* time with each family member. Have at least one meal together each day and use this time to talk about what each person did that day. If dinner doesn't work, try breakfast.

2. Couple time: Set at least two appointments to meet and talk with your spouse each week. Use one to discuss routine business, such as servicing the car, fixing the roof, or changing money markets. Use the other for romance. The best time for the rendezvous is when the children are in bed or staying over at a friend's house. See if a trusted relative or neighbor will take over so you can get away for a romantic weekend. If you can't afford the trip, see if you can send the kids to grandma's and turn your home into a romantic bed-and-breakfast for a couple of days.

3. Personal time: (Yes, you need time for yourself.) Increase your personal time by learning how to say no to things that you don't *have* to do and don't *want* to do. Find even more time by getting up a half hour earlier—before everyone else gets up—or by going to bed a half hour later. Go to work earlier or leave later, and use that time for yourself.

4. Home/car/yard time: Hire someone else to do the work. Get a junior high student to help around the house. Better yet, delegate chores to your children and spouse. Develop a flexible cleaning schedule, and don't fret if the house isn't squeaky clean. Learn to live with comfortable clutter. Make a photocopy of your master shopping list, and shop by phone or computer as much as possible. Set up a meal schedule that includes easy-to-make dinners and healthy take-out on your busy nights.

5. Job time: Plan ahead for each work day, and budget your time properly to avoid taking work home. If you work at home, realize that it's okay to close the office door so that you can concentrate on your work—provided that the little ones are being monitored by another adult!

6. Friends time: Schedule time for friends. Have lunch or coffee two or three times a month. Friendships are important to your emotional and mental health, especially during stressful times.

7. Community time: Limit your community time to what you can handle, but try not to stop it altogether. By serving your community, you're acting as a positive role model for your child.

But increases in quantity don't have to precede improvements in quality. Here are some ground rules for enhancing the quality of whatever time you have with your child:

- Only make promises you can keep. And keep every promise you make. This builds trust.
- Smile. It shows your love.
- Listen when your child speaks, and let her disagree with you now and then. This helps to build respect.
- Talk about rules and responsibilities so that your child knows your expectations. State consequences up front and be fair. Value equal treatment of self and others without favoritism or prejudice.
- Let him make mistakes, and help him to learn from those mistakes.
- Promote independence, and allow for privacy.
- Do things together, even if you only have small amounts of time. Pop some popcorn. Go window-shopping. Make a lunch date. Watch a DVD.

- Be spontaneous. Have a pillow fight. Make a snowman. Blow bubbles.
- Use your car time together as an opportunity to talk (but don't use it just for interrogating or preaching).
- Share emotional events, both happy and sad. Be open to your child's feelings, even if they don't match your own. Don't criticize or take offense at what he says. When you encourage your child to open up and express his feelings, you let him know that feelings are important. Take the time to talk about your own feelings. This helps him to identify his own feelings.
- Show common courtesy by using words such as *please* and *thank you*.
- Ask her about her day, and tell her about yours.
- Encourage him to follow his interests. Express your pride in his accomplishments.
- Be there for her school events, plays, sports games, and other special events.
- Tell him that you love him, and give him plenty of hugs and kisses. As your child gets older, he may be embarrassed by this type of attention in front of his friends. That doesn't mean that he won't want to cuddle just before bedtime when his friends are nowhere in sight.
- Your teenagers need less undivided attention, but they still need your time and love. Since there are fewer opportunities for you to get together, make sure to be there when they do want to talk or get involved in a family activity. Attend concerts and other events with them or go shopping at the mall—provided they'll allow it! Many teens don't want to be seen in public with their parents, but they still value some one-on-one time with mom or dad.

To show your love and attention most effectively, cultivate closeness. Closeness grows through physical proximity, eye contact, conversation, and touch, and it can occur during everyday activities as well as during scheduled events. You can't force closeness, but you can try to be open to and take advantage of the opportunities that present themselves. To close this chapter, here are fifty ways to cultivate closeness with your child:

1. Give him a hug.
2. Tell her that you love her.

3. Learn about his Matchbox® cars.
4. Be silly together.
5. Play her favorite games with her.
6. Listen to his favorite songs with him.
7. Ask her about her day.
8. Set limits.
9. Listen to his stories.
10. Be honest.
11. Have a tea party.
12. Go for a ride in her cardboard box "car."
13. Share his excitement.
14. Stay with her when she's afraid.
15. E-mail him a "thinking of you" card.
16. Giggle and laugh together.
17. Delight in her inventions.
18. Praise that mud pie.
19. Thank him.
20. Laugh at her jokes.
21. Answer his questions.
22. Let her teach you something.
23. Have a soda with him and his friends.
24. Give her a special nickname.
25. Let him make decisions.
26. Ask her to tell you something she knows that you don't.
27. Give him lots of special time.
28. Celebrate special events, like the first day of school.
29. Trust her.
30. Applaud his successes.
31. Inspire her creativity.
32. Bake cookies together.
33. Let him choose the dinner menu sometimes.
34. Have a pizza party.
35. Go out for ice cream.
36. Put happy notes in her lunchbox or backpack.
37. Go for a walk together.
38. Introduce him to your friends.
39. Take her out for a lunch or other gathering with your friends.
40. Take him to your work for a day.
41. Display her crafts where everyone can see them.
42. Tuck him in.

43. Read together.
44. Watch a movie together.
45. Attend her special events.
46. Visit his school.
47. Accept and celebrate her for who she is.
48. Share a secret.
49. Believe what he says.
50. Daydream with her.

2

HEALTH

Child death rates dropped significantly over the last twenty years, and respiratory illnesses, especially the common cold, remain the leading cause of childhood morbidity. However, a 2001 Policy Statement from the American Academy of Pediatrics notes that our increasingly complex environment brings newer childhood concerns such as the following: school and learning problems, child and adolescent mood and anxiety disorders, the alarming increase in adolescent suicide and homicide, firearms in the home, school violence, drug and alcohol abuse, human immunodeficiency virus and acquired immunodeficiency syndrome (HIV/AIDS), and the effects of media on violence, obesity, and sexual activity. Recent evidence compiled by the World Health Organization indicates that by the year 2020, childhood psychiatric disorders will rise by over 50 percent to become one of the five leading causes of illness, death, and disability among children. We still have time to change that outcome. Children have the need to be healthy, physically and emotionally.

*****

Children's health problems, issues, and challenges have undergone alarming changes since I first began working with children over thirty years ago. HIV/AIDS has grown to be one of the leading causes of death in children. More and more children suffer from disorders once thought not to affect them—depression, suicidal thoughts, and anxiety disorders. I've seen preschoolers admitted to psychiatric hospitals because of the severity of their illnesses and children as young as eight die from complications of eating disorders. And we've all seen far too many kids diagnosed with attention-deficit/hyperactivity disorder (ADHD).

HIV/AIDS

Human immunodeficiency virus (HIV) causes a broad range of diseases, with acquired immunodeficiency syndrome (AIDS) being the most severe. Child and adolescent AIDS accounts for only 1–2 percent of all reported AIDS cases in the US, yet HIV infection is a leading cause of death in infants and children one to four years of age. AIDS prevents the body's immune system from effectively fighting disease. A child with HIV/AIDS is vulnerable to "opportunistic" illnesses such as serious infections, and since children have immature immune systems to begin with, almost any organism can be opportunistic, including the common childhood infections.

Most children become infected via mother-to-infant (vertical) transmission through the placenta, during delivery, or possibly through breast feeding. Vertical transmission cases have decreased 80 percent because of effective preventive treatment. Adolescents develop HIV/AIDS in the same ways adults do—through sexual contact or through sharing contaminated needles (drug use, unhygienic tattooing and body piercing). Approximately ten thousand adolescents are infected with HIV each year. HIV cannot be transmitted by casual contact such as kissing, coughing, sneezing, shaking hands or sharing meals; nor is it transmitted via toilet seats, swimming pools, food or drinking water.

Pediatric HIV differs from adult HIV in several ways: 1. The time between infection and diagnosis is shorter in infants and young children, as most untreated infants develop symptoms by their first birthday. 2. Disease symptoms in children include physical and developmental failure to thrive. 3. Children experience early opportunistic infections, a greater number of bacterial infections from childhood illnesses, and lymphoid interstitial pneumonitis (LIP), a condition in which the child may be asymptomatic or could have saliva gland enlargement, clubbed fingers, shortness of breath, coughing and/or eye inflammation.

4. Pneumocystis carinii pneumonia (PCP) can occur as early as within two months of birth. 5. The Centers for Disease Control and Prevention (CDC) classifies HIV infection as mild, moderate or severe in children under thirteen years of age.

Mother-to-infant transmission can be greatly minimized by medicating infected mothers during pregnancy and delivery and then treating the newborns. Adults and adolescents can minimize their risk by utilizing the suggestions on the following web sites:

- National Institutes of Health - www.ashastd.org
- Centers for Disease Control and Prevention - www.cdc.gov/hiv
- American Academy of Family Physicians - www.familydoctor.org

There is also information immediately available at the CDC Info Line. This toll-free number is 1-800-CDC-INFO (1-800-232-4636).

OBESITY

With an increased incidence of 25 percent over the last twenty-five years, obesity now ranks as the most common childhood nutritional disorder in the US. Obesity is defined as an excessive amount of body fat—greater than 25 percent of total body weight in boys and greater than 32 percent in girls. Another way to ascertain body fat is the body mass index or BMI, which is calculated using a person's weight and height. In children, a BMI that exceeds the 95th percentile for age and sex indicates obesity—a problem easy to diagnose but difficult to treat.

The BMI was recently recommended as an additional measure of growth for children and as an indicator of body "fatness" and potential weight problems. Thus, you will soon see your child's BMI measured and charted right along with his height and weight. You can calculate your child's BMI now by going to the Centers for Disease Control and Prevention's page on Body Mass Index for Children at: http://www.cdc.gov/nccdphp/dnpa/bmi/bmi-for-age.htm and clicking on the BMI calculator in the upper right hand corner. Type in your child's information, submit it, and get his BMI automatically. You can also access the Child and Adolescent BMI charts to see where your child's BMI fits in.

Childhood obesity has been associated with numerous health problems. An obese child has a higher blood pressure, heart rate, and cholesterol levels than non-obese kids, and these can lead to heart disease.

The excess weight increases the chances for orthopedic problems, such as bow-legs, slipped hip, and weight stress on their leg joints. It also makes them more prone to skin disorders, especially heat rash. A fungal infection can develop in their skin folds, creating the suspicion of Type II diabetes. Many obese children and adolescents have impaired glucose tolerance, a condition that often appears before the development of Type II diabetes.

Obesity unleashes the potential for poor self-esteem, negative self-image, withdrawal from peers, and depression. Children learn at a very early age to stigmatize obese people as stupid, lazy, slow, and self-indulgent. Research shows that children prefer a playmate who is disabled or wheelchair-bound to one who is obese. Psychological stress from obesity can be especially difficult during adolescence when peer acceptance is a crucial component of development and identity.

The causes of obesity are more complex than they seem and include genetic, biological, familial, and environmental factors. Less than 10 percent of childhood obesity is associated with a genetic or hormonal defect, such as Turner's syndrome, Prader-Willi syndrome, or hypothyroidism. Children with these disorders typically exhibit other symptoms, such as short stature and mental impairment, and they rarely have a family history of obesity. These disorders can be diagnosed by your children's healthcare provider via a careful history, physical examination and laboratory tests.

Most overweight children have idiopathic (undetermined cause) obesity. They gain weight because their energy input (diet) exceeds their energy output (basal metabolic rate), in other words, they take in more calories than they burn. It takes 3,500 calories to gain one pound; therefore, an excess intake of only 50 to 100 calories per day can lead to a five to ten pound weight gain in just over a year. A relatively small imbalance between inputs and outputs can lead to a significant weight gain over time. Most obese children gain their weight slowly over a period of years.

Heredity can influence the response to overfeeding, regional fat distribution, and general 'fatness.' Babies born to overweight mothers have been found to be less active and to gain more weight by age three months than babies born to normal weight mothers. This suggests there may be an inborn drive in the babies of overweight mothers to conserve energy. For children who are genetically predisposed to obesity, preventive intervention may be the best course of action. But it's not all genetics. There are other factors involved in obesity.

As already noted, a disorder such as hypothyroidism can cause obesity, as can some medications, including steroids and antidepressants. Another important biological factor is the "set point." Each of us has a weight that the body will defend, the weight that it keeps coming back to after dieting. That weight is called the set point.

Parents pass genes to their children, but they also pass down habits and fixed patterns associated with diet and activity. When parents demonstrate poor eating and exercise behavior, they indirectly affect their children's behavior—present and future. Most cultures place great value on food, not only for its nutritional value, but also for its role in social occasions and celebrations. However, when food symbolizes comfort or reward, it can lead to excessive dietary intake. Eating can become a response to anxiety, boredom, frustration, and depression. Family instability and other stressors can have a negative effect on children's self-esteem, causing them to overeat and risk obesity. As children gain weight, social pressures may mount as they get teased and bullied, prompting them to continue to turn to food for comfort.

Regardless of genetics, environmental factors play a significant role in childhood obesity. Most cases of obesity result from too much food and too little exercise. And bad influences are ubiquitous:

- Food ads are everywhere—TV, movies, billboards, magazines and newspapers.
- Supermarkets lure you to the higher priced, frequently not-too-healthy foods. How often do you walk in and face a stack of yummy baked goods? Notice that the expensive, sugar-laden cereals are directly at toddlers' eye level as they sit in shopping cart seats? Both supermarkets and discount chains have candy at almost every checkout.
- "Super-sized" means just that—a huge amount, not an average serving. But we like to get more for our money, and since it costs only pennies more to get the giant size portion, we give in, over and over again, until our eyes forget what a normal portion is. Do you feel cheated because the cereal box claims to hold sixteen servings, and you can only get four? If you said yes, you have super-sized eyes! Fortunately, most fast-food chains have begun to eliminate their super-sized items.
- Soft drinks and sugar-laden fruit drinks that pass for juice contain few or no nutrients, yet kids down them regularly. Even fruit juice can add to obesity when consumed in large quantities—consump-

tion of 12 ounces or more a day has been associated with obesity in preschoolers.

• Sedentary lifestyle contributes to obesity, and studies show that 48 percent of girls and 26 percent of boys do not exercise vigorously on a regular basis.

• The prevalence of obesity is higher in kids who watch four or more hours of television per day. Television slows the metabolism of mesmerized couch potatoes, and children are more likely to snack on high-calorie junk food while watching TV.

Some children are more prone to obesity than others. If your child has any of the following risk factors, make sure he gets proper nutrition and exercise:

• Has a parent who is or was obese
• Spends a lot of time involved in sedentary activities
• Does not get enough exercise
• Watches TV or plays video games for more than two to four hours per day
• Consumes a large number of calories at a time
• Has little parental supervision
• Gets bored easily

Obesity should be treated as a disorder. Your child needs a complete examination from her healthcare provider who will first determine whether the weight gain is a symptom of another physical illness. If not, then she needs a program that creates lasting weight loss through reduced calorie consumption and increased exercise. Your healthcare provider can help you make sure that your child is able to handle dietary change and exercise safely.

According to obesity specialist Rebecca Moran, MD, successful weight loss programs contain five main components: reasonable goals, dietary management, physical activity, behavior modification, and family involvement.

SUCCESSFUL WEIGHT LOSS PROGRAMS

Reasonable goals For weight loss goals to work, they need to be attainable and allow for normal growth. Set both short- and long-term goals. Short-term goals should start small so that your child doesn't get discouraged—lose one pound per week, or five per month. Her long-term goal can be the total amount of weight loss needed or the ability to easily perform a previously difficult or impossible task, such as walking up a flight of stairs without getting out of breath.

Dietary management   A nutritionist can develop a sensible dietary program that will allow for both weight loss and normal growth. One pound of weight equals 3,500 calories. So the diet will need to eliminate 500 calories per day to achieve a one pound per week weight loss. This diet should provide the recommended percentages of protein, carbohydrates and fats that your child needs. He should also consume an adequate amount of fiber to increase his feeling of fullness and to displace fat in his diet.

Make sure he eats a healthy breakfast–cold cereal with fruit and milk or whole wheat toast with peanut butter. Failure to do so can result in binge eating, as well as his doing poorly in school. Keep healthy snacks handy. Choose from different food groups (apple with peanut butter, milk with graham crackers), and discourage empty calories from cookies, chips, and candy. He doesn't have to give up fast foods completely, but he should be smart both in making choices and in making sure they fit into his daily calorie plan.

Physical activity   Your child needs physical activity to maintain weight and redistribute fat. After getting approval from your health-care provider, start your child off slowly to avoid discouragement. Start with a five minute walk or bike ride and work up to twenty or thirty minutes of physical activity per day, in addition to the exercise she gets in school.

Behavior modification   An essential for lifestyle changes, behavior modification for weight loss includes self-monitoring, stimulus control, modification of eating patterns, and positive reinforcement. Your child can monitor his own eating and exercising patterns by keeping a diary that documents the time, the amount and type of food eaten, and the amount of exercise performed. This will force him to have more awareness of how much he actually eats and how little he exercises.

Stimulus control means limiting the things that stimulate your child to eat, including sitting in front of the TV. Limit TV time and don't allow eating while watching. TV isn't the only stimulus to eating.

Many children eat when stressed or bored. To help identify your child's stimuli, have her document the circumstances that surround eating.

Without the help of a diary, this girl's parents might not have realized that her negative eating behaviors resulted from her being bullied at school.

Help your child modify his eating behavior by encouraging him to sit, take smaller bites, chew the food longer and put his fork down between bites. Reward him for positive behavior, but don't use food as a reward. Give ample praise for reaching goals. Occasional tangible rewards, like a trip to the mall, or some new sporting equipment, can give an extra boost. Avoid negative reinforcement. Telling your child that he's fat and depriving him of food when he's hungry will only damage his self-esteem and may lead to rebound weight gain.

Example of the diary your child should keep to document circumstances around eating:

My diary

6:30 woke up and got ready for school

7:00 ate breakfast: 1 bowl of cheerios with milk and a glass of orange juice

7:30 got on school bus, sat in the back. Totally gross.

8:00 started school

12:00 lunch time. That mean kid picked on me again. She wouldn't let me sit at my favorite table and made fun of me because I'm fat. I was so embarrassed that I couldn't eat my lunch

3:00 got home. Mom's still at work and I'm hungry! Ate 2 peanut butter and jelly sandwiches with chocolate milk and only about 8 cookies. But it's okay, right, I didn't eat any lunch, right?

Family involvement   Long-term weight loss requires active family involvement and support. Without nagging, actively work with your child on her weight loss plan. And remember, she learns by watching what you do. If your diet and exercise patterns lead you to gain weight, she may follow suit, regardless of the intensity of her weight-loss program.

Weight-loss medications are not recommended for children. Neither are surgical procedures such as gastric bypass. However, some commercial programs, including Weight Watchers and Jenny Craig, accept children (with parental and medical permission). Check the white pages of your phone book for centers near you.

Losing weight is never easy, and maintaining weight loss can be an even bigger challenge. But the consequences of obesity remain severe, while the benefits of weight loss are worth the challenge.

EATING DISORDERS

Eating disorders, particularly anorexia nervosa and bulimia nervosa, are serious, complex, chronic disorders that can be life threatening. They usually begin during adolescence and disproportionately affect females. About 3 percent of young women have an eating disorder. But only 10 percent of people with eating disorders are male. (Anecdotes also report eating disorders in prepubertal children.)

Anorexia Nervosa has been called the relentless pursuit of thinness. Affected individuals refuse to maintain a body weight at or above a minimally normal weight for their height and age. They weigh less than 85 percent of their normal weight for their height, build, and age, yet they firmly believe that they're overweight. Anorexics have intense fear of gaining weight or becoming fat, even when underweight. There is also a disturbance in the way they experience their body weight and or shape. This body-image disturbance can range from a mild distortion to a severe delusion and is not related to the degree of weight loss. These teens may be preoccupied with their entire body or a specific body area, such as the abdomen, thighs, or buttocks.

Bulimia Nervosa is charaterized by chaotic eating patterns. Bulimic individuals have recurrent binge-eating episodes during which they eat a relatively large amount of food in a short period of time, feeling out of control during the binge. These episodes are accompanied by repeated compensatory mechanisms to prevent weight gain, including self-induced vomiting, laxative and/or diuretic abuse, ipecac (a medication used to induce vomiting) abuse, fasting, and excessive exercise. Like anorexics, bulimics are constantly concerned with their body shape and weight.

Bulimic teens develop an intense preoccupation with food that progressively interferes with their educational, vocational, and/or social activities. Shame follows their bingeing, and they're usually quite distressed by their binge and purge behavior. Bulimic teens are also at risk for impulsive behaviors such as substance abuse, shoplifting, and promiscuity, increasing their chances for chemical dependency, criminal prosecution, and sexually transmitted diseases, including HIV/AIDS.

In both disorders, thinking is concrete and somewhat superstitious, causing many such teens to see things in an all-or-none/black-or-white fashion—"If I eat one cookie, I'll have to eat the whole bag." "If I don't get an A in this course, I might as well fail it." Eating-disorder teens also have a high incidence of associated psychological problems, including substance abuse, obsessive-compulsive disorder, personality disorders, depression and suicidal thoughts. Death from eating disorders is usually due to electrolyte (body salt) imbalance, starvation, or suicide.

Binge-Eating Disorder is a recently recognized problem that features episodic uncontrolled consumption, without compensatory activities, such as vomiting or laxative abuse, to avert weight gain. Binge-eating disorder is probably the most common eating disorder. Most people with this problem are either overweight or obese, but it also occurs in normal-weight people. About 2 percent of all adults in the US have binge-eating disorder, including about 10–15 percent of people who are mildly obese and who try to lose weight. It's even more common in people who are severely obese. Binge-eating disorder is a little more common in women than in men.

Eating disorders can cause a host of physical complications. Children with anorexia can develop heart, liver, and kidney damage from malnutrition. Their pulse and blood pressure drop, occasionally causing dizziness and fainting. They lose their periods (or don't start them if prepubertal) because of decreased body fat and low estrogen. These, along with low calcium intake, can lead to osteoporosis long before middle age. Anorexics can't concentrate and may be moody and withdrawn.

Although extreme bingeing can lead to stomach rupture, most complications of bulimia come from purging. The combination bingeing and purging causes "chipmunk cheeks,"—enlarged saliva glands caused by overuse from bingeing, and irritation by the stomach acid bath from vomiting. At the least, self-induced vomiting can cause dental decay, but it can also lead to erosion of the esophagus and serious electrolyte imbalance, particularly potassium depletion, which can produce fatal heart problems. Some bulimics resort to using ipecac to induce vomiting. (You may be familiar with this drug because your healthcare provider may have had you keep it on hand in case of accidental poisoning in your toddlers.) Bulimics, however, tend to take massive doses, which can prove fatal—ipecac overuse is toxic to the heart. Some bulimics resort to other purgative measures to lose weight, including laxative or diuretic (water pill) abuse, diet pills, and enemas. Any of these can lead to problems, such as dehydration and electrolyte imbalance.

The causes of eating disorders remain unknown, but they are considered to have individual, familial and sociocultural factors. Eating disorders tend to be noted more often in girls with poor self-esteem, in families where other family members have eating disorders, and in cultures that emphasize the desirability of being thin. Eating disorders aren't contagious, but susceptible teens can be easily influenced by friends who think that being thin is the most important thing in the world.

As mentioned, culture plays an important role in the development of eating disorders, which have flourished in industrialized nations since Twiggy made her debut in the 1960's. Unfortunately, things haven't gotten much better. The media still projects an image that equates success with thinness. The thin woman—be she actress or supermodel—gets the job, the guy, the car, the house and the bucks. Add to this the multibillion dollar dieting industry, which advertises heavily, and teens are constantly bombarded with a distorted version of reality. The undistorted version is that 98 percent of women are larger than supermodels and that inner beauty is more important than outer.

How would you know if your child is at risk for developing an eating disorder? Your child has a higher risk than average if she fits any of the following:

- Has low self-esteem and is easily influenced by others
- Is interested in being a dancer, cheerleader, model, actress or other thin-oriented profession
- Is an athlete, particularly a runner
- Is a perfectionist who is eager to please
- Has trouble controlling her impulses
- Has few friends
- Thinks that dieting will make her feel better about herself

- Has been physically or sexually abused
- Has a family member with an eating disorder

Males are at greater risk if they are gay, wrestlers, or jockeys.

Eating disorders are not as obvious as obesity. The following are signs that your child may have an eating disorder:

- She experienced a recent weight loss or weight fluctuations of more than five pounds.
- She exhibits a fear of gaining weight or of being fat.
- She has a preoccupation with being fat, or focuses on a specific body part.
- She shows signs of purging behaviors—she goes into the bathroom right after meals (to vomit); she has a scrape or scar on her knuckles (from sticking her fingers down her throat to induce vomiting); you have found laxatives or diuretics hidden in her room.
- She has a distorted image of her body's size or shape.
- She exhibits a preoccupation with thoughts of food, calories and her weight.
- She has restrictive eating patterns, such as skipping meals, fasting, or eliminating entire food groups.
- She shows a preference for eating alone.
- She is preoccupied with food related items, such as cookbooks
- She tells others what to eat and comments on the calorie content of family members' food.
- She reports a loss of periods or has a delay in the onset of puberty and menarche (first period).
- She is underweight.
- She exercises compulsively, or gets upset if her exercise ritual is broken.
- She shows extreme denial about weight loss and evidence of her eating disorder.
- She withdraws from friends and family, or has very superficial friendships.
- She wears bulky clothing to hide weight loss.
- She is shoplifting.
- She steals items or money to buy food.
- You discover that large quantities of food regularly go missing.

Eating disorders require professional treatment. If you suspect that your child has an eating disorder, contact your healthcare provider.

ANXIETY DISORDERS

For many children, fear becomes phobia, and anxiety turns to anxiety disorder. Youngsters with anxiety disorders are usually so afraid, worried, or uneasy that they can't function normally. These disorders can last a long time and, if left untreated, can interfere greatly with your child's life.

Although very common, anxiety disorders in children are often overlooked or misjudged. Since a certain level of anxiety is normal, it becomes important to distinguish between normal levels and pathological levels of anxiety. The experience of anxiety often has two components: physical components, such as headache, stomachache, and sweating, and emotional components, which include nervousness and fear. Anxiety disorders, on the other hand, often affect a child's thinking, decision-making ability, and perceptions of the environment. Anxiety disorders can cause a number of physical symptoms, including diarrhea, shortness of breath, high blood pressure, and heart palpitations. They are frequently accompanied by other disorders, such as depression and substance abuse.

Anxiety disorders are true illnesses, not figments of the imagination. The ones commonly seen during childhood are: generalized anxiety disorder, adjustment disorder with anxiety, separation anxiety disorder, obsessive-compulsive disorder, specific phobias, social phobia, panic disorder, acute stress disorder and post-traumatic stress disorder.

GENERALIZED ANXIETY DISORDER (GAD)

GAD is defined as excessive worry, anxiety, and apprehension occurring most days for a period of six months or more. The worries are diffuse, covering a number of topics and events. These children have difficulty controlling their anxiety, which is associated with some of the following: feeling on the edge or pent up; restlessness; getting easily fatigued; having trouble concentrating or feeling "My mind goes blank;" irritability; muscle tension; and sleep disturbances. This anxiety causes serious distress or problems functioning.

ADJUSTMENT DISORDER WITH ANXIETY

Most often, adjustment disorder with anxiety occurs within three months of a specific stressor, such as a move, change of school, or parental divorce. The child experiences feelings of anxiety, nervousness, and worry. These are signs of—marked distress in excess of what would be expected from the situation—that can seriously impair his social or academic performance. The problem usually dissipates six months after the initiating stressor ceases.

SEPARATION ANXIETY DISORDER

A child with separation anxiety experiences intense anxiety, sometimes to the point of panic, when separated from a parent or other loved one. Separation anxiety typically appears suddenly in a child who had no previous signs of a problem. The anxiety is so severe that the she cannot perform daily activities. When separated, she becomes preoccupied with morbid fears of harm that will come to her or fears that her parent(s) will not return. Separation anxiety can give way to school phobia—child will refuse to go to school because she fears separation from her parent(s).

OBSESSIVE-COMPULSIVE DISORDER (OCD)

Once thought to occur only in adults (think Melvin Udall in "As Good as it Gets" or Adrian Monk), OCD is now more frequently diagnosed in children. It is characterized by persistent obsessions (intrusive, unwanted thoughts, images, or urges) and compulsions (intense, uncontrollable, and repetitive behaviors, or mental acts, related to the obsessions). These obsessions and compulsions cause distress and consume huge amounts of time. The most common obsessions involve dirtiness and contamination, repeated doubts, and/or the need to have things a specific way. Others include fearful aggressive or murderous impulses and disturbing sexual images. Frequent compulsions include repetitive handwashing, using tissues or gloved hands to touch things, touching and counting things, checking locks, repeating actions, requesting reassurance, and performing counting rituals.

Children with OCD become trapped in the cycle of repetitive thoughts and actions. Even though they realize that their thoughts and behaviors appear senseless and distressing, it seems they cannot stop repeating them.

SPECIFIC PHOBIA

Specific phobia is an excessive, persistent fear that is objectively unreasonable and is triggered by specific objects: (snakes, spiders, computers), or situations (close spaces, heights, flying, being injured). Exposure to one of these immediately provokes anxiety. The distress is so severe that it interferes with the child's functioning or routine.

SOCIAL PHOBIA

A very common phobia, social phobia is the persistent and substantial fear of one or more social situations in which a child is exposed to unfamiliar people or scrutiny by others. During these situations, he feels that he will behave in a manner that will be embarrassing or humiliating. Exposure to these situations causes significant anxiety and even panic, despite his knowing that the fear is unreasonable. This fear can cause a child to avoid such situations, leading to marked interference in life.

PANIC DISORDER

Panic disorder consists of recurrent panic attacks—sudden, discrete episodes of intense fear that are usually accompanied by a desire to escape and a feeling of impending danger or doom. These usually peak within ten minutes, subside in twenty to thirty minutes, and are accompanied by at least four of the following: palpitations, sweating, shortness of breath or feeling smothered, trembling or shaking, sweating, nausea and abdominal pain, dizziness, lightheadedness, feeling faint, a sense of unreality or of being detached from one's self, fear of losing control or of going crazy, numbness and tingling, and chills or hot flashes.

ACUTE STRESS DISORDER AND POST-TRAUMATIC STRESS DISORDER

In both acute stress disorder and post-traumatic stress disorder, a child is exposed to a traumatic event in which she experiences, witnesses or is confronted by a situation—abuse, violence, or a natural or man-made disaster—that involves an actual or perceived threat of serious injury or death. The child's response can involve intense fear, helplessness, or horror, and she may relive the event in recurrent images, thoughts, and/or dreams. She may in situations that resemble the event, feel intense anxiety or believe that the event is recurring. She may also experience some of the following: inability to remember details of the event, increased participation in activities, feelings of detachment, restricted emotional range, difficulty making decisions, irritability, agitation, anger, resentment, numbness, spontaneous crying, and a sense of despair. Acute stress disorder occurs within two days of the event and lasts less than one month. Conversely, post-traumatic stress disorder commonly has a delayed onset and lasts *more* than a month.

As with most psychiatric disorders, the exact causes of anxiety disorders are unknown. However, several factors have been implicated:

- Anxiety disorders can be the result of a combination of internal and external stresses that overwhelm a person's coping abilities.
- About 50 percent of people with panic disorders have at least one relative who has an anxiety disorder, and there is an increased chance of a child developing an anxiety disorder if his parent or sibling has one.
- Certain brain chemicals and abnormal brain functions have been implicated in the development of anxiety disorders. Evidence supports the involvement of imbalances in the brain chemicals norepinephrine, GABA, and serotonin. This helps to explain the success of using medications to treat many of these disorders.
- Certain illnesses, such as lung and endocrine disorders, can lead to anxiety disorders. Therefore, all children with anxiety symptoms should be checked for underlying medical problems, such as asthma and hyperthyroidism. Some medications, including some used to treat asthma, may also result in anxiety symptoms.

Researchers found that a child's basic temperament may play a role in developing an anxiety disorder. A child who tends to be very shy and restrained in unfamiliar situations may be at risk. Researchers also suggest monitoring for signs of anxiety between the ages of six and eight, when imaginary fears should diminish, but a child may be excessively anxious about school performance or social relationships.

Everyone gets anxious from time to time, and we all have our fears. However, excessive anxiety suggests that your child should be evaluated by a professional. Talk to your healthcare provider if your child exhibits any of the following:

- She has difficulty concentrating.
- He becomes more active or less active than usual.
- She eats a lot more or a lot less than usual.
- He regresses back to earlier behaviors (such as thumb sucking.)
- She has trouble sleeping.
- He complains of stomachaches, or headaches.
- She wets or soils her pants.

Anxiety disorders require professional treatment, which may include individual and/or family psychotherapy, medications, and environmental treatment.

MOOD DISORDERS

The most common mood disorders found in children and adolescents are major depressive disorder, reactive depression, dysthymia, and bipolar disorder. Mood disorders such as depression increase the risk for suicide, which reaches its peak during the adolescent years. About two-thirds of children and adolescents with depression also have another mental health disorder, such as an anxiety disorder, a disruptive or antisocial disorder, an eating disorder, or a substance abuse disorder.

MAJOR DEPRESSIVE DISORDER

Major depression is a serious condition, that has many symptoms similar to those seen in adults. It is characterized by one or more major depressive episodes that last from seven to nine months. A child with this disorder becomes extremely sad, losing interest in the activities that normally please her most. She criticizes herself and believes that others criticize her. She feels pessimistic, helpless and unloved. She experiences difficulty making decisions, has trouble concentrating and may neglect her appearance and hygiene. Feelings of hopelessness can arise and evolve into suicidal thoughts or actions.

Depressed children and teens are often irritable and sometimes become aggressive. Some teens feel a surge of energy, and occupy every minute of their day with activity to avoid the depression. Depressed youths may become anxious and have separation fears, and they may have somatic complaints such as headaches, stomachaches, and other aches and pains.

REACTIVE DEPRESSION

Also know as adjustment disorder with depressed mood, reactive depression is the most common form of depression in children and teens. This depression is usually short-lived and is a response to an adverse experience, such as rejection, a slight, a letdown, or a loss. Children can develop reactive depression to a divorce, a death, a relationship breakup, moving, or changing schools.

DYSTHYMIA

Dysthymia is similar to major depression but with fewer symptoms and a more chronic course. Because of its persistent nature, dysthymia tends to interfere with normal development. A child with dysthemia feels depressed for most of the day, on most days, and for several years. The average duration of symptons is four years. Some are depressed for so long, they don't recognize their state as abnormal. Therefore, they don't complain of being depressed.

Characteristics of dysthymia include low energy or fatigue, changes in eating and/or sleeping patterns, poor concentration, and a feeling of hopelessness. About 70 percent of these children will eventually experience an episode of major depression.

BIPOLAR DISORDER

Also called manic-depressive disorder, a child (or teen) with bipolar disorder has episodes of depression and mania, with depression usually occurring first. The manic stage may not appear for months or years later after a symptom-free period. Mania may be expressed with unusual energy, poor judgment, euphoria and feelings of grandiosity, or it may appear with irritability and aggression. A manic child is overconfident, and talks rapidly, loudly, and excessively. He can't sleep, rarely eats, and feels that his thoughts are racing. He does things quickly in a creative but chaotic, disorganized manner. He may experience delusions of great self-importance and invulnerability, engaging in risky behavior, such as careless sex or fast driving.

SUICIDE

Although somewhat unusual in younger children, suicide is not uncommon in teenagers. As a matter of fact, it's the third leading cause of death in people ages fifteen to twenty-four, and the rates for younger teens are rising. Females attempt suicide more often than males, but males are more successful in actually committing suicide because they use more lethal means.

Most victims of suicide have a psychiatric illness, usually major depression or bipolar disorder. Other victims have severe anxiety, exhibit violent and impulsive behavior, have no plans for the future, or are deficient in social skills. Most suicides, both the attempted and the successful, have a precipitant, such as experiencing a relationship breakup, family or school violence, rejection, or sexual abuse. Other precipitant's include causing a pregnancy or getting pregnant, and contacting or spreading a sexually transmitted disease. Abuse of drugs and/ or alcohol and the availability of deadly weapons plays a key role in suicide. Another key factor can be exposure to the suicide of a friend or family member. ("Copycat" suicides remain common among teenagers.)

Your child is at increased risk for suicide if any of the following are true:

- He has previously attempted suicide. (The risk is greater if this happened within the past three months.)
- She has a psychiatric disorder.
- A family member has a mood disorder.
- A friend or family member has committed or attempted suicide.
- He or a family member has a substance abuse problem.
- There is family discord.
- She exhibits impulsiveness, hostility, and/or poor social skills.
- He has problems with school, including truancy.
- She has a recent relationship breakup
- He takes unnecessary risks.

If any of these apply to your child, talk to a healthcare provider.

Some warning signs call for an immediate response. Immediately bring your child to an emergency facility if you see or hear any of the following:

- He says or implies he wants to hurt or kill himself.
- She has a suicide plan.
- He exhibits irrational speech.
- She shows signs of a sudden alienation from the family.
- He shows a sudden interest or loss of interest in religion.
- She hears voices or sees visions.

- He gives his possessions away.
- She writes notes or poems about death.
- He is preoccupied with death-themed music, movies, art or video games.
- She expresses feelings of hopelessness.
- He makes statements such as, "You won't have to worry about me anymore."

Mood disorders can be successfully treated with therapy or medication. If you suspect that your child may have a mood disorder call your healthcare provider or contact a mental health service near you. You should be able to locate one in the blue pages of your phone book.

3

SAFETY

The new millennium brings the dangers that past generations couldn't imagine: Internet predators, abductions, date violence, terrorist attacks, weather disasters, and school shootings. Today's children live with these perils, as well as move mundane hazards involving vehicles, fire, water, poisons, or drugs. Children have an essential need to be safe from harm. It is our responsibility to protect them and show them how to protect themselves.

*****

The evening began as any other as they prepared for bed. Mom carried their seven-month-old. Dad was in the shower. Their two-year-old daughter toddled into her parent's bedroom. As mom turned off the lights, she heard a loud noise. Investigators believe that the TV, cable box, VCR and dresser fell on the toddler when she attempted to climb them. The little girl's death came just ten days after a New Jersey boy died after becoming trapped under a TV set. He died on what would have been his eighth birthday.

Unintentional injury is the most significant, (yet largely unrecognized) public health threat facing children today. It is the leading cause of childhood deaths. The number of accidental deaths is staggering, but it pales when compared to the number of children who are hospitalized, who require emergency treatment, and who suffer permanent disability due to accidental injury. The economic burden to society is astounding, reaching billions of dollars annually. Astounding too, are the emotional loss, suffering, and pain a child and family endures once an injury has occurred.

Sometimes injury is not accidental. No decent human being can comprehend why anyone would intentionally injure children, but it happens. Children can be victimized by their peers, abductors, molesters, Internet predators, and even by their own parents. (Homicide is the fifth highest cause of death in children.)

ACCIDENTAL INJURY

The type and severity of injury are closely related to a child's developmental stage, and his physical, intellectual, and psychosocial needs and skills. For example, a young child's skin is less mature than an adult's, predisposing the child to more severe burns. Accidents can happen when the demands of a particular task exceed the ability to complete the task. A preschooler can safely navigate stairs that represent a danger to a toddler. However, that same prescooler cannot safely cross the street alone. Risks increase as a child becomes more physically proficient and curious. A school-age child engages in more activities away from home, and an adolescent can drive a car.

Research does not support the idea that some individuals are naturally "accident-prone." But some children are at higher risk for accidents than others. Boys have a higher risk for injuries, especially during their teen years, as do children with delays in their development of intellectual and/or motor skills. Other children at risk are those who exhibit behaviors such as risk-taking, aggression, and hyperactivity, or who have poor self-esteem.

Gibson noted that there are five environmental agents in all injury events, and these are the five forms of physical energy—mechanical, chemical, thermal, electrical, and radiant. Haddon built on this, dividing injury into three phases: 1) the pre-injury phase when the person loses control of the energy source; 2) the injury phase when energy is transferred to the person who is then injured; and 3) the post-injury phase when attempts are made to repair the injury.

Several other factors are key determinants of accidental injury. Urban kids face different hazards than rural kids do, but rural accidents are more likely to be fatal. Stress, unemployment, substance abuse, single-parent households, and poverty influence injury rates. Poor children have a twofold increase in injury deaths, a fourfold greater risk of drowning, and a fivefold greater risk of fatal injury from fire. Native Americans have the highest per capita injury rates, followed by African Americans, Caucasians, and Asian Americans. Behavioral changes have helped reduce injury. These include the use of seatbelts, child safety seats, bike helmets, child-safe caps on medication bottles, and fire-retardant clothing.

MOTOR VEHICLE ACCIDENTS

Of all the accidental deaths in children from birth to nineteen years of age, 47 percent are attributable to motor vehicle accidents. Although motor vehicle accidents remain the leading cause of accidental death in children ages one to nineteen, accidents involving other vehicles add to the fatality statistics, resulting in more than eight thousand childhood transportation fatalities in the year 2000 alone. Bicycles, skateboards, scooters, and all-terrain vehicles (ATVs) contribute to the death and injury toll. A child can be an accident victim in his own driveway or while walking on the sidewalk, and he can even be injured by a shopping cart.

Motor vehicle safety starts with you. When looking for a new car, consider a model with a wider wheel base as these provide greater protection for passengers in the event of an accident. Drive with caution at all times. Heed the speed limit, and don't drink and drive. Drive defensively, not aggressively—your child depends on you. Follow these safety guidelines:

- Keep your car maintained, and make sure your tires are properly inflated.
- Plan ahead, so you don't have to rush.
- Keep your eyes on the road. Remain alert. If you're tired, don't drive.
- Use your seatbelt and lock the car doors. Use safety seats and seatbelts as appropriate for your child.
- Strap or stow objects that could become missiles in a sudden stop.
- Don't speed. Don't weave in and out of traffic. Don't cut other drivers off.
- Don't follow too closely. Keep a safe distance from traffic in adjacent lanes.

- Slow down and use your lights in work zones.
- Follow the rules of the road.
- Use your turn signals when turning or changing lanes. Yield the right-of-way.
- Avoid road rage: take a deep breath, count to ten, and remember your kids are with you.
- Carry a cell phone for emergencies, (but DON'T use it while driving).
- Keep a first aid kit and emergency equipment handy.

Remember, following these guidelines will not only increase your child's safety today, but sense he is watching you, someday soon he will be copying what he has seen.

Unfortunately, many parents believe that they can leave a child in the car while they run "quick" errands. Quick is never quick enough, and a delay of just a few minutes can prove fatal. Heat rises rapidly inside a car, even when the windows are slightly open. The temperature can rise from 93° to 125° in twenty minutes, and to 140° in forty minutes. Such heat is more dangerous to a child than to an adult because it can rapidly overwhelm the child's physical ability to adjust. The temperature of a young child can rise three to five times faster than that of an adult in the same enviroment. A child can go into shock, causing vital organs to fail. Never, never leave your child in a parked car when the weather is warm.

In a crash involving a pickup truck, passengers who ride in the cargo bed are three times more likely to die than are the occupants of the cab. And a disproportionate number of cargo bed riders are youths. Since the cargo area isn't designed for passengers it is neither designed nor required to meet occupant safety standards. Forty-eight percent of cargo bed rider fatalities were children; 9 percent of these children were under age five. Children who ride in the cargo area are more likely to sustain severe or multiple injuries in an accident. Fatality rates are also higher for children than for adults in that situation. The most significant hazard is ejection, even without a crash, as a child can be ejected due to a sudden stop, swerve, or turn. Children can also be injured by jumps or falls from the cargo area. Nearly one-third of cargo area passenger deaths were the result of non-crash events.

Pedestrian injury is the second leading cause of injury-related deaths in children ages five to fourteen. While most of these are traffic related, children under age two are most likely to suffer from non-traffic related injuries involving vehicles, including those occurring in driveways or parking lots, or on sidewalks. Children are at high risk for pedestrian-related injuries because they are exposed to traffic threats that may exceed their thinking, behavioral, physical, and/or sensory skills. Children are impulsive, and have problems with judging speed, distance, velocity, and spatial relations.

Adults generally tend to over estimate a child's skills as a pedestrain. Your child's auditory and visual acuity, depth perception and proper scanning ability develop gradually and do not fully mature until ten years of age. Don't let your child cross the street alone if she's under ten-years-old. She needs adult supervision until she fully develops her pedestrain-in-traffic safety skills.

Motor vehicle accidents remain a leading cause of death in adolescents—two out of five deaths among US teens result from motor vehicle accidents. Results from the 2003 Youth Risk Behavior Surveillance (YRBS) indicated 18.2 percent of high school students had rarely or never worn seat belts—that's up from 14.1 percent in 2001. The survey also revealed that during the thirty days prior to the survey, 12.1 percent drove a car or other vehicle after drinking alcohol and 30.2 percent had ridden with a driver who had been drinking alcohol. Many adolescents view a license as a right of passage and/or a passport to freedom rather than as a tremendous responsibility to provide safe transportation for themselves and others. Teens are more likely to engage in risk-taking behavior, and they lack driving experience. All of these increase their risk of crashing and sustaining injuries or worse.

Protect your teens by doing the following:
- Treat driving as a privilege with responsibilities, not as a birthright.
- Establish that you—not your teens—control the car keys and the use of the car.
- Ensure the mechanical safety of your car(s) and have your teens participate in the maintenance, even if that just means accompanying you to the mechanic's garage.
- Set a good driving example and follow all traffic rules.
- Require that your teens maintain good grades to keep their driving privileges. (Ask your auto insurance company if they have a "good student" discount.)
- Remind your teens how easy it is to get distracted on the road. Encourage them to stay focused when driving. (Minimize conversation. No horseplay. All cell phones off.)

- Enforce restrictions, such as banning certain passengers, limiting the number of riders, and always returning the car with not less than a half tank of gas.
- Create rewards for safe driving (increased driving time, a free tank of gas), as well as consequences for unsafe driving (decreased driving time, loss of driving privileges).
- Don't tolerate drinking and driving. But let your teens know that you will pick them up if they do drink—no questions asked (until the following morning).
- Be alert to any signs that indicate that they are drinking or using drugs.
- Support programs that make driving safer for teens (graduated license laws: minimum drinking age laws, safety belt laws, curfews, educational efforts to teach teens about safe driving habits, safe ride programs so teens won't drive after drinking at parties).

DROWNINGS

Childhood drownings and near-drownings can happen in minutes. A child loses consciousness two minutes after submersion and suffers irreversible brain damage in just four to six minutes. Fully 92 percent of the children who survive are found within two minutes of submersion, and 86 percent of the children who die are discovered after ten minutes. Nearly all the children who require CPR and survive are left with severe brain damage. But, since CPR does benefit some children, it remains prudent for you to learn it. Contact your local American Red Cross or American Heart Association for a training program near you.

About 350 children under age five drown in swimming pools each year. Pools rank as the number one cause of drowning in preschool-age children and pose a danger to all children. Teens should know how to swim, but they're more likely to take risks, overestimate their skills, or combine swimming or poolside activities with drug and alcohol use. They can also underestimate water depth and the strength of currents when diving or swimming in water bodies such as lakes and rivers. To keep your children safe, use guidelines suggested by the American Red Cross, National Safe Kids Campaign, the American Academy of Pediatrics, and SafeKids:

- Learn to swim. If nothing else, you'll be setting a good example.
- Learn CPR. And learn other ways to help a drowning victim.

- Teach your child to swim when she is old enough, usually by age five.
- If you own a pool, make sure that it is adequately fenced and gated to prevent children from sneaking in when it's unattended. Empty all wading pools and put them away when not in use.
- Keep electrical appliances away from the water.
- Do not allow playing with or riding wheeled toys, running, or clowning around near the water.
- Never let your child swim without adult supervision, and be sure the supervising adult knows how to swim, how to get emergency help, and how to perform CPR.
- Never leave your child unsupervised near pools, spas, tubs, wells, open post holes, irrigation and drainage ditches, or other bodies or water.
- Don't rely on inflatable toys and mattresses to assist your child in floatation, and don't allow him to use these toys if he can't swim.
- Never use floatation devices or inflatable toys and mattresses in place of supervision.
- Warn your child of the risks of drowning or hypothermia that could result from her breaking through thin ice in the winter.
- Obey all rules and posted signs.
- Pay attention to weather forecasts and don't allow swimming when the forecast calls for thunder or lightning.
- Watch for the dangerous "too's:"—too cold, too tired, too much sun, too far from safety, and too much strenuous activity.

Not all drownings occur in pools or lakes. Small children can drown inside their homes, and many of these deaths are associated with common household products. The Consumer Product Safety Commission provides these examples:

1. About two-thirds of the drowning deaths in the home occur in bathtubs. Some of these deaths involve a child who was in a bath seat or ring. Most of them occur when the parent isn't present. Stepping out to answer the phone, check on dinner, or grab a towel can prove fatal.
2. Five-gallon buckets, often used for household chores, pose a serious threat to toddlers. Fifty-eight children under the age of five died this way in 1999 alone. The tall, straight sides of the bucket, combined with its stability, make it nearly

impossible for a top-heavy infant to free himself when he topples in headfirst. For those who still use them, diaper pails can also be a drowning hazard.

3. Toilets are often overlooked as a drowning hazard in the home. The typical scenario involves a child under three-years-old falling headfirst into the toilet. Keep the lid closed.

4. Spas or hot tubs pose another drowning hazard. A solar cover can allow a baby to slip into the water while the cover appears to stay in place, hiding the infant.

Spas and hot tubs present other hazards to children, including burns from the chemicals used to clean the water, stress from higher water temperature to children under five, burns from the water temperature to very young children, electrical shock or electrocution when an electrical current comes into contact with the spa or tub, and injuries from slips and falls.

---

5. Home ponds and fountains, both inside and out, and rain barrels are also drowning hazards.

Don't assume your house is safe. Check for all potential hazards, and correct them.

BURNS

Household fires can result in smoke inhalation, devastating burns and death. The rate of fire-related injuries among children has declined since the seventies, but fire and burns remain the fourth leading cause of injury-related death in children age fourteen and under. Children under five are particularly susceptible to fire-related death because they a have a less acute perception of their environment and a limited ability to react promptly and properly. Rural children have a greater chance of dying in a home fire as death rates in rural areas are twice the rates of deaths in big cities and three times higher than in small towns.

More than 43 percent of at-home fire-related deaths are of children under nine who die trying to escape. A child in a fire may become unable to act or may act irrationally. Having an escape plan might reduce the number of such deaths, yet only 26 percent of households develop and practice escape plans.

Children under age four and children with disabilities have the greatest risk of burn-related injury or death. Their risk is highest for scald and contact burns. Boys are at greater risk than girls. Boys, ages ten to fourteen, are particularly at risk for fireworks injuries. (Children under four are at greater risk for sparkler injuries.) And any child in a home without a smoke alarm is at the greatest risk for fire-related injury and death.

Hot water causes thermal injury, and tap water hotter than 120°F causes 24 percent of scald burns in children under four. You can greatly reduce the risk of Scalding by setting your water heater thermostat to 120°F (48°C).

Burns come from a number of thermal, electrical or chemical sources: wood stoves, kerosene heaters, space heaters, grills, hot liquids, cooking equipment, irons, hair-curling equipment, electrical cords, cigarettes, matches, fireworks, and the sun. To keep you children safe from burns, follow these suggestions from the US Fire Administration, the National Safe Kids Campaign, the American Academy of Pediatrics, the Hearth, Patio and Barbeque Association, the New York City Fire Department, and the US Consumer Product Safety Commission:

- Install and maintain UL-listed SMOKE DETECTORS on each level of your home and outside every sleeping area. For extra safety, install one inside each sleeping area, too. Follow the manufacturer's directions, test them once a week, and change their batteries twice a year or if they "chirp" for a battery change. Don't "borrow" the smoke detector batteries to operate anything else. Never disconnect the battery to stop the "chirping".
- Keep Fire extinguishers handy, and know how to use them. Even though they come in many shapes and sizes, all are similar to operate.

The Hanford Fire Department, operated by the US Department of Energy, suggests remembering the PASS acronym for fire extinguisher use:
- P = PULL the pin (at the top of the device) that keeps the handle from being accidentally pressed.
- A = AIM the nozzle at the base of the fire.
- S = SQUEEZE the handle to discharge the extinguisher. Stand eight feet away from the fire. (The discharge will stop when you release the handle.)
- S = SWEEP the nozzle back and forth at the base of the fire.

- Once the fire appears to be out, monitor it carefully to make sure it doesn't re-ignite.
- Develop and practice an ESCAPE PLAN in case of fire. Plan at least two ways out of the house (preferably two ways out of each room) and choose a meeting place outside where all will gather. Practice the plan regularly and often. Your child may become frightened and confused during a fire. Having practiced different scenarios, she will be more likely to escape harm.
- If your home has a second level, obtain a noncombustible fire escape ladder, and practice using it. Apartment buildings should have safe, functioning fire escapes. Create a specific plan if your child has disabilities. Consult your local fire department for help. If your child is deaf or nonverbal, teach your neighbors to use and understand the sign language sign for fire. And be sure to teach the fire escape plan to all your child's caregivers, including babysitters.
- In case of fire, crawl low on hands and knees under the smoke to exit a room. Use stairs to exit a building. Never use elevators—they can stop on a burning floor. Instruct your child to STOP, DROP, ROLL, and COOL if his clothing catches on fire.
- Teach all children ages 3 and older what to do in case of a fire. Tell them that the sound of a smoke alarm means to go outside to the meeting place.

RURAL SAFETY

Children living in rural areas have a much higher risk of accidental injury-related death than do children living in urban areas. They're especially at risk from drowning, motor vehicle crashes, firearm injury, residential fires, and agricultural work-related injury. Higher injury fatality rates in rural communities are due in part to the high number of farm-related injuries. Children account for 20 percent of all injury-related farm fatalities and represent an even larger portion of nonfatal injuries. Injuries in rural settings occur in remote, sparsely populated areas that usually lack trauma care, resulting in prolonged response and transport times. The short supply of medical facilities, equipment, and personnel also contributes to increased risk.

Children should always be supervised when performing work-related farming tasks, and should never perform tasks that are inappropriate for their age, size, strength, cognitive ability, or prior experience.

They should also be prevented from entering hazardous areas. National Agriculture Safety Base of the CDC provides age-appropriate information for parents and grandparents regarding the safety of children on the farm:

- TODDLERS AND PRESCHOOLERS: Injuries to toddlers and preschoolers tend to occur when they are playing on the farm or riding on farm equipment. Toddlers and preschoolers can climb, walk and run. They have very short memories and like to test reality. Preschoolers have a fascination with moving parts, such as power takeoff belts (PTO's) and grain augers. Children under five learn by trial and error. Typical farm accidents for toddlers and preschoolers include the following: falling from tractors; falling from heights (from silos or ladders), or through hay holes; being kicked and stepped on by animals; and ingesting chemicals.

- Here are some safety tips:
  - Never have a child as an extra rider on a tractor.
  - Keep ladders out of reach.
  - Keep chemicals in locked storage.
  - Supervise a preschooler's activities.
  - Provide a fenced play area away from farming activities.

- SCHOOL-AGE CHILDREN: Injuries to school-age children occur at both work and play. This is the age when a child likes to explore and be creative and when parental attention and praise are very important. A school-age child generally tries to complete any assigned task to please his parents, even when the task may not be appropriate for him. He may not feel he can say no even if he knows the task is beyond his abilities. This can result in accidents. Typical accidents involving school-age children include the following: falling from heights; being pinned or crushed during tractor roll-overs; being entangled in machinery; and suffocating in grain.

- Here are some safety tips:
  - Restrict play areas.
  - Carefully evaluate your child's physical and mental maturity for a given task.
  - Have proper protective devices on equipment, such as roll-over protective structures, seatbelts, and shields.
  - Place warning decals on hazardous equipment or in dangerous locations.

- Discuss farm dangers with your child on a regular basis—make safety "JOB 1".

- ADOLESCENTS: (Ages twelve to sixteen) Most teens participate in farm labor. Therefore, their injuries are usually work-related. Teens are greatly influenced by peer pressure. They don't want to look like failures. They want to impress others. They tend to believe they're immortal. Many risky behaviors, intended to impress, can result in accidents. Typical accidents involving teens include the following: tractor roll-overs; amputations from PTO's; motor vehicle accidents; and suffocation in grain bins.

Age should not be used as the sole measure of maturity. Some other variables that distinguish individual adolescents are judgment and body size. Experience and observation help to improve judgment. A parent who models proper safety precautions is the best teacher. Improper behaviors that a parent performs automatically, such as stepping over a moving PTO, will likely be copied by his teenager. There is tremendous variation in size among adolescents. Growth occurs in spurts and varies between siblings. A task that was appropriate for one child at age twelve, may not be appropriate for a brother or sister at the same age.

- Here are some more safety tips to follow:
  - Evaluate your child's physical and mental maturity for a given task.
  - Install the proper protective devices on equipment.
  - Have your child complete the necessary safety course before operating farm machinery.
  - Teach her to use personal protective equipment.
  - Discuss farm safety with her on a regular basis.
  - Ask questions to reinforce the importance of safety precautions. Keep safety first.
  - Be a good role model.

No matter what age your child is, you must be aware of his development. When assigning a task, consider your child's age, maturity level, attention span, and physical size. If your child isn't physically ready for a task (for example, if he's too short), don't allow him to perform it. Don't alter machinery in an attempt to make up for your child's developmental state, a (e.g., using blocks on tractor brakes). Assess his level of alertness. If your child has been in school all day, he may be tired. Fatigue will increase the likelihood of an accident. A little time spent evaluating capabilities before assigning tasks may prevent an accident or may even save your child's life.

FIREARMS

Every day in America, ten children are killed in handgun suicides, homicides, and accidents, and for every child killed, four are wounded. The firearm death rate for fifteen to nineteen year-olds increased more than threefold from 1984 to 1994. The non-firearm homicide rate actually decreased almost 13 percent. With over 200 million guns, the United States is the most heavily armed country in the world and the only industrialized country in which handguns are widespread and easily available. In just one year, guns killed no children in Japan, 19 in Great Britain, 57 in Germany, 109 in France, 153 in Canada, and 5,285 in the United States.

Many criminologists believe that handgun availability is related to the high rate of homicide in this country. Most victims of assault by other weapons do not die, but the death rate from assault by handgun is extremely high. Research indicates that of all firearms, handguns are the murder weapon of choice, and that the people at greatest risk of being murdered by handguns are teens and young adults.

Firearm injuries are already the second leading cause of death among young people ten to twenty-four years of age. They may soon be the *leading* cause of deaths, outranking motor vehicle accidents. Firearm death already ranks as the leader in the District of Columbia and in five states (Alaska, Louisiana, Maryland, Nevada, and Virginia). An estimated twenty thousand people a year are paralyzed by handgun wounds, creating lifetime medical costs that parallel the polio epidemic of the 1950's. In all, firearm violence costs Americans about one hundred billion dollars a year.

One of the surest ways to keep your child away from guns is to keep guns out of your home. However, many children are raised in homes with guns, particularly if family members engage in hunting or target shooting. Almost half of all American households with children have one or more guns. And, unfortunately, there's a gun left hidden but unlocked in one of every eight family homes. If you don't own a gun, understand that your child probably knows someone whose parents do own one. He could come into contact with a gun at a neighbor's house, when playing with a friend, or under other circumstances.

When you make a decision to own a gun, don't make it lightly. Be fully aware of the risks gun ownership could create for you and your family. Learn the dangers of firearms, teach your children about these dangers, as well as nonviolent ways to deal with anger and conflict. Practice firearm safety. Always remember that the life you save may be you child's.

Here are some firearm safety tips:
- Keep all firearms—handguns, sporting guns, antique guns, BB guns, pellet guns, nail guns, and others—unloaded and safely locked up in a gun safe, fire safe, or lockbox. Loaded guns don't belong inside bedroom drawers (where far too many people keep them). The manner in which you store your gun can be a matter of life and death. A variety of devices exist for securing your gun. Safes seem to provide the most security, but many people prefer gun locks, which you can obtain for free or at low cost. Look for the gun-lock distribution program in your area.
- Never allow your child access to a gun without adult supervision.
- Store and lock ammunition in a separate location where your child cannot access them.
- Keep the keys for both the gun(s) and the ammunition out of your child's reach, in a place different from where you store your other household keys.
- Talk to your child about guns and gun safety. Nail guns, BB guns, air guns, handguns—all are possible for your children to obtain, and all are dangerous. At some point, your child will come into contact with some type of gun, so talk to him and teach him about gun safety. Be open, honest, and clear. Avoid statements such as, "Stay away from guns," and "Don't even think about going near the gun cabinet," without explaining your reasoning and giving him the opportunity to ask questions.
- Teach your child the following safety steps from the National Rifle Association (NRA) Eddie Eagle Gun Safety Program:
  - If you find or see a gun of any kind—
    - STOP!
    - Don't touch.
    - Leave the area.
    - Tell an adult (parent, neighbor, teacher, police officer, or other trustworthy adult).

INTENTIONAL INJURY

Accidental injuries greatly outnumber intentional injuries; but intentional injuries remain a leading cause of childhood deaths. And it's a sad fact that most murdered children are killed by a parent. Child abuse isn't the only source of intentional injury to children. Children are also injured and killed by others through youth violence, abduction and child molestation.

CHILD ABUSE

The term child abuse denotes one or more acts of commission or omission by a caregiver that prevents a child from actualizing his potential growth and development. Approximately 10–20 percent of children ages three to seventeen are abused each year. Child abuse includes the following: physical abuse—the intentional act of injuring a child; *Shaken-baby syndrome is a form of physical child abuse that affects between twelve hundred and sixteen hundred children every year.* Munchausen Syndrome by Proxy—the fabrication or inducement of illness by one person onto another (usually by a mother to a child); emotional abuse—the deliberate attempt to destroy a child's self-esteem or competence; neglect—the deprivation of necessities such as food, water, and shelter, or the failure to meet a child's need for attention, affection and emotional nurturing; and sexual abuse—contact or interaction between an adult and a child where the child is used for sexual stimulation of the adult.

Children who experience abuse are at increased risk for adverse health effects and behaviors as adults. These include smoking, alcoholism, drug abuse, eating disorders, severe obesity, depression, suicide, sexual promiscuity, and certain chronic diseases. Abuse during infancy or early childhood can cause important regions of the brain to form improperly, leading to physical, mental, and emotional problems such as sleep disturbances, panic disorder, and attention-deficit/hyperactivity disorder (ADHD). A person who in childhood has been physically assaulted by a caregiver is twice as likely to be physically assaulted in adult life. As many as one-third of parents who were abused in childhood may go on to victimize their own children. The direct costs (law enforcement, judicial, and health system responses to child abuse) are estimated at twenty-four billion dollars each year. The indirect costs (long-term economic consequences of child abuse) exceed an estimated sixty-nine billion dollars annually.

If you are reading this book, chances are you're not an abusive parent. But you may know someone who is, or you may just want to help prevent this tragedy. Child abuse has many causes, and there is no easy formula for prevention. But here are some general prevention strategies that you can support in your community:

- teaching parents about child development, parenting skills, self-control, and anger management
- providing respite care for stressed parents, and helping them access support—housing, food, healthcare, transportation, counseling, and other community resources
- teaching children self-protection
- providing support, counseling and other needed services (emergency care, foster placement) for abuse victims

YOUTH VIOLENCE

We painfully acknowledge the epidemic of violent behaviors in children—explosive tantrums, fighting, threats, weapon use, vandalism, animal cruelty, firesetting, date violence, and homicide. Homicide ranks as the second leading cause of death in children ages fifteen to nineteen, and the leading cause of death for African-American and Hispanic youths in the same age range.

Although children can be born with problems such as low intelligence and impulsivity, they are not born violent. They learn violence at home and in their community. Homes can be breeding grounds for violence when parents engage in abusive behaviors, are overly strict in their discipline, and/or use corporal punishment. But even in the best of homes, children can learn violent behaviors from the violent people around them and from violence in the media. Children who witness violence can see it as a way to solve problems and may tend to become violent themselves.

The first step in preventing violence is identifying the factors that place children at risk. Research demonstrates that violence is multifactorial, that is, there are a number of influences that may lead a child to become violent. According to the Centers for Disease Control and Prevention (CDC), childhood violence involves four clusters of factors:

1. Individual factors include a history of preschool aggression, beliefs supportive of violence, social and intellectual deficits, and poor emotional attachment to caregivers.

2. Family factors include poor monitoring or supervision, and exposure to violence, abusive behavior, overly strict discipline, and parental substance abuse.
3. Peer/social factors include associating with peers engaged in high-risk or problem behavior, who have a low commitment to school and experience academic failure.
4. Neighborhood factors include poverty and lack of economic opportunity, high levels of transiency and family disruption, and exposure to violence.

Mitigating factors—empathetic and loving caregivers, parental supervision, high self-esteem, a sense of responsibility, positive role models, problem-solving abilities, strong communication skills and social skills, good peer interactions, tolerance, and a sense that one is in control of one's life—seem to make children less likely to be one violent.

The National Youth Violence Prevention Resource Center suggests the following tips for parents to help prevent youth violence:

- Give your child consistent love and attention.
- Communicate openly with your child, and encourage her to talk about all aspects of her life.
- Set clear standards for your child's behavior, and be consistent about rules and discipline.
- Make sure your child is supervised.
- Promote non-violent conflict resolution by being a good role model.
- Talk to your child about the consequences of drug abuse, weapon use, gang participation, and violence.
- Limit your child's exposure to violence in the media.
- Limit your child's exposure to violence in the home or community.
- Take the initiative to make your school and community safer.

ABDUCTIONS

Every year, between 1.3 and 1.8 million children are reported missing in the US. Some children may be lost; some have run away from home. Some are kidnapped by their noncustodial parent or relative, and some are taken by strangers. Still others disappear leaving few clues as to why or how. Unfortunately, a recent survey by the National Center for Missing & Exploited Children showed that not enough parents know the information that can be vital in the recovery of an abducted child.

The National Incidence Studies of Missing, Abducted, Runaway, and Throwaway Children (NISMART) describes a nonfamily abduction as an episode in which someone from outside the family abducts a child through physical force or threat of bodily harm, or detains a child for at least an hour without parental authority or lawful permission. Or it could be an episode in which a child younger than 15 or mentally incompetent is detained or voluntarily accompanies a nonfamily perpetrator who takes the child, conceals the child's whereabouts, demands ransom, or expresses the intent to keep the child permanently.

A stereotypical nonfamily abduction occurs when a child is detained overnight, transported at least 50 miles, held for ransom, abducted with intent to keep the child permanently, or killed by a stranger or slight acquaintance. A stranger is a perpetrator who is unknown to the family or who has an unknown identity, and a slight acquaintance is a perpetrator whose name is unknown to the child or family prior to the abduction and whom the child or family didn't know well enough to speak to, or a recent acquaintance who the child or family knows for less than six months or known for longer than six months but seen less than once a month.

Most high profile cases are stereotypical abductions—children are abducted, sexually assaulted, and killed. However, not all nonfamily abductions are stereotypical. Most children are abducted by people they know—babysitters, boyfriends, ex-boyfriends, grandparents, classmates or neighbors. Some are detained for short periods of time, as when one child confines another in the school bathroom to sexually assault her, or when a babysitter refuses to let a child go home because the parent hasn't paid for prior babysitting duties.

The majority of abductions by strangers take place in streets, parks, wooded areas, highways, and other places easily accessible to the general public. Abductions by acquaintances typically occur in the home, but 25 percent of these kidnappings take place in public places. Strangers or acquaintances rarely abduct from schools or school grounds.

If your child were missing, could you accurately describe her? The FBI tallies twenty-one hundred new missing-children reports every day. Of course, these can be more easily solved when parents are able to provide descriptive information. Too many parents lack the vital information needed to find their child in those crucial first hours. Don't be one of them. Be prepared for the unthinkable:

- Keep a complete up-to-date description of your child, including her date of birth, height, weight, hair and eye color, and other identifying characteristics (birth marks, braces, glasses, body piercings, tattoos).
- Take an ID photo of your child every six months—every three months if she is under two. Head and shoulder photos, taken from at least two different angles, are preferable to school and family pictures.
- Know where your child's medical records are located and know how to access them. Make sure they contain information that can help in identifying your child.
- Make sure your child has up-to-date dental records and know how to access them.
- Have your child fingerprinted by your local police department and keep the fingerprint cards in a safe place. The police will NOT keep those records themselves.
- Consider having your child's DNA tested. Fingerprints provide accurate identification, but sometimes DNA information is more useful. For more information on DNA testing and how to get your child tested go to www.dnafiler.com or www.kids-dna.com. Both sites offer at-home testing kits.

PREVENTING NONFAMILY ABDUCTIONS

Being prepared is not enough. You and your child need strategies to prevent abductions:

- Make sure your child knows his full name, address and phone number(s). An older child should also know his parents' names, work addresses, and work phone numbers.
- Keep communication lines open. Don't belittle your child's fears or concerns.
- Talk to your child. Kids who talk regularly with their parents have higher levels of self-esteem and are more self-assured, making them less vulnerable to predators.
- Be sensitive to changes in his behavior.
- Don't let him wear clothing with his name on it. A perpetrator can use your child's name to gain his confidence.
- Set boundaries as to where your child can go. A young child should not leave the yard unsupervised. An older child should ask permission. A teen should phone home to tell you where she is.

- Establish a parental back-up system so your child has somewhere to go in an emergency.
- Instruct your child to tell you if an adult asks her to "keep a secret" or if someone offers her money, gifts, or drugs, or asks to take her picture.
- Tell him that adults don't usually ask children for directions or for help finding a puppy or kitten.
- Instruct her not to go near the car of a person who tries to talk to her. Your child should learn which cars she may ride in. Share a password with her known only to family members.
- Tell him to go for help—police station, neighbor's house, store—if someone is following him on foot or in a car.
- Carefully choose babysitters, nannies, daycare providers, preschools, and after-school programs. Check references, and see if you can have access to their background information. Several states will allow you to access criminal and sex abuse registries.
- Know your child's friends and their parents.
- Know your neighbors.
- If someone demonstrates a great deal of interest in your child, find out why.
- Beware of gadgets that promise to keep your child safe. These may lead to a false sense of security that may actually heighten the risk of abduction.
- Don't rely on martial arts or self-defense training to keep your child safe. (Martial arts training may, however, build his confidence and self esteem.)
- Teach on-line safety. (www.safekids.com)
- Be sure your child know that if she is home alone, she should not answer the door or tell anyone that she is home alone.
- Tell him to say NO! to anyone who tries to take him somewhere, touches him, or makes him feel uncomfortable in any way.
- Instruct her not to go into anyone's home without your permission.
- Have a family plan in case you and your child become separated while away from home.
- Tell him not to look for you if you become separated while in a public place or shopping area. He should go to the nearest check-out counter, security office, or lost and found, and tell an offical he's lost. He should never go to the parking lot without you.
- Instruct her to scream, "You're not my parent!" or "Fire!" if someone tries to take her away.

CHILD MOLESTATION

The legal definitions of sexual abuse, assault and exploitation vary from state to state, but most definitions include sexual contact, the abuse of power, and the nonconsent of the victim. Children, by nature of their age, are not able to give consent. Incest is any form of sexual contact between a child and an immediate family member (parent, stepparent, sibling, stepsibling), extended family member (uncle, aunt, cousin, grandparent) or surrogate parent (adult whom child views as a family member). A child can be abused by someone outside of her family (usually someone she knows), or by another child—typically an adolescent who has been victimized himself. Child sex abuse can include contact but it might not. Contact forms of abuse include fondling the child's genitals, masturbation, oral-genital contact, digital penetration, and vaginal and anal penetration. Noncontact forms of abuse are exposure, voyeurism, and child pornography. Despite the impression we get from media coverage, few molesters abduct, rape, and murder their victims.

Child molesters come in all shapes and sizes and from all socioeconomic groups. They may be janitors or, CEOs. There is no typical child molester, but some characteristics of the crime are clear: Sexual abuse is the perpetrator's exploitation of power and authority. Most victims are molested by someone they know. The majority of victims are female. The majority of abusers are male. Child pornography is strongly linked to child molestation.

Although molesters vary, they can be categorized as being either preferential molesters or situational molesters. Preferential molesters, or pedophiles, are sexually attracted either exclusively or in part to prepubescent children. Even their fantasies revolve around children. Situational molesters engage in sex with children for a variety of reasons—some connected to stress and substance abuse. Some situational molesters commit the act only once, while others have a life-long pattern of child sexual abuse that makes them difficult to distinguish from pedophiles. Many pedophiles date single mothers to get access to their children, while others hang around playgrounds for the same reason. Pedophiles also tend to take jobs or volunteer in occupations that involve children.

Child abuse can occur in a wide range of settings and situations. Long-term abusers typically "court" a child with attention, affection, and presents, essentially seducing her. Other abusers use fear or bribery. Abuse occurs by either coercion or force, and the child is told to keep it a secret or is threatened with harm should she tell about the abuse. The child may feel guilty or ashamed about the abuse. (This may hamper disclosure.) When caught by the justice system, many pedophiles claim that the child initiated the sexual activity, or that the child wanted to do it.

Children who become victims of sexual abuse may consequently suffer from emotional and behavioral problems ranging from mild to severe that can be either short-term or long-term. Typical problems include stress disorders, guilt, depression, anxiety, fear, withdrawal, acting out, and sexual dysfunction. Revictimization is common—when they become adults, sexually abused children are more likely to be victims of rape or to be victims (and/or perpetrators) in physically abusive relationships. Although all children are potential victims, some are at greater risk than others. Those at greater risk include in the following:

- He is a loner, or a runaway.
- She lives in a home where other forms of family violence occur.
- He has a parent who has been abused.
- She lives in a geographically isolated area.
- He lives in family that exhibits extreme mistrust of outsiders.
- She lives in a family that is overly close, has poor communication skills, and keeps potentially volatile "family secrets."

Many parents have difficulty talking about sexual norms and values with their children. Most parents find discussing sexual abuse even more difficult. But your child's ignorance can contribute to disaster. If your child can't recognize it, how will she know if she's being sexually abused? Given that 25 percent of all girls and 13 percent of all boys are sexually abused before age eighteen, you have an obligation to protect your child by providing the necessary information. Child victims often feel that they have caused the abuse. Your child needs to know ahead of time that there's nothing wrong with her and that abuse is the problem of the perpetrator not the victim. Although you can never completely protect your child from sexual abuse, you can do your best to minimize her chances of being abused:

PRESCHOOLERS

- Teach her the proper names for body parts, including genitals and breasts.
- Tell her that no one—strangers, friends, or relatives—has the right to touch her private parts (parts coved by a bathing suit) or to hurt her.
- Tell her it's okay to say NO! to people who make her feel scared, uncomfortable, or embarrassed.
- Instruct her to tell you if an adult asks her to keep a secret.
- Keep a close eye on her—a preschooler can be easily fooled by a perpetrator.

SCHOOL-AGE CHILDREN

- Give him straightforward information about sex.
- Reinforce that his body belongs to him and that no one has the right to touch his private parts.
- Explain that some grown-ups have problems and are confused about sex and that such an adult may try to do things that make him feel uncomfortable.
- Teach him personal safety—to get away from any adult who makes him feel fearful or uncomfortable.
- Tell him to come to you immediately if such an adult bothers him.

TEENAGERS

- Explain that unwanted sex is an act of violence, not an act of love.
- Discuss rape and date rape.
- Reinforce her right to say NO!.

Be sure to teach your child the safety techniques discussed in the abduction section (pp. 51–54) as well. But remember, sexual abuse can occur under your own roof by family members, friends, or babysitters. So keep the lines of communication with your child open at all times. Listen to her and be alert for unusual behaviors from her and from others in and around your household.

Keeping children safe leads to a safer world for all of us!

Part Two
Enrichment Needs
(Social)

4

FAMILY

The family is the primary social unit for a growing child. So a strong and stable family is vital in nurturing a child's spiritual, emotional, and social development. Unfortunately, today's families face enormous pressures. Outside demands on time, energy, and finances can stress family members and strain family resources. But every child has an essential need for family strength and stability. So we adults are responsible for creating and maintaining families that will nurture and grow happy, healthy children.

*****

According to the 2000 census, Scranton, Pennsylvania has a population of 76, 415. It is by most definitions a big city. But this old coal mining town still rightly takes pride in its roots and old-fashioned community values. With a mean age of 38.8 and an average household income of $28, 805, Scranton is hardly a place I would expect to find gangs. Yet the US Office of Juvenile Justice and Delinquency Prevention lists Scranton as one of many US cities that reported active youth gangs in the 1998 Youth Gang Survey.

No longer limited to cities like Los Angeles, gangs are growing, with the Crips, Bloods, and their offshoots sprouting in cities, suburbs, and rural areas across the country. Why do kids join gangs? Some join for the parties and drugs, some for protection from other gangs. Some look for respect. Many join in search of a family.

A report by Herbert G. Lingren entitled, *Gangs: The New Family*, notes that family problems and parenting difficulties can increase the risk of kids joining gangs—and many of these kids do come from troubled middle-class families with both biological parents at home. These kids are looking for the acceptance, love, companionship, leadership, encouragement, recognition, respect, role models, rules, security, self-esteem, structure, and sense of belonging that are lacking in their own households. Family does not have to be kin.

FAMILY DEFINED

US families have passed through major transitions. Once self-contained, cohesive domestic work units, they have become groups of persons dispersed among various educational and work settings. Other nonfamily groups have taken over functions handled by families. Schools educate, hospitals care for the sick, churches give religious training, government and private companies build and manage recreational facilities, nursing homes care for the elderly, and mortuaries prepare the dead for burial. Businesses even prepare meals and provide clothing.

Technology and societal changes influence family definition, structure, roles, and responsibilities. But technological advances alone can't determine family structure and function. Families adapt to and resist outside pressures. In today's disposable society, where people can feel uneasy and dispensable, individuals seek secure relationships. Although for some children, families are anything but secure, families are usually still the primary source of security.

Though definitions vary, the term family usually refers to a small social system made up of two or more persons living together who are related by blood, marriage, or adoption, or who live together by agreement over a period of time. Family units are characterized by face-to-face contact, emotional and financial commitment, cooperation, competition, and mutual concern. They share goals, identity, behaviors, rituals, and a history—a continuity of past, present, and future. (Of course, the concept of family may be understood differently within different cultures.)

Both external and internal structures shape a family. External structures include religion, culture, social class, environment, and the extended family. Internal structures include family composition, rank order, subsystems and boundaries. Family composition varies from house to house. Today, less than 25 percent of US households are nuclear families—the traditional biological mom and dad with 2.5 children. Other forms include the following:

- Single-parent families – One parent is responsible for the care of the children as the result of death, divorce, desertion, birth outside marriage, or adoption.
- Reconstituted families (or stepfamilies) – One or both parents have children from previous marriages.
- Blended families – Step parents have at least one child born within the new marriage.
- Binuclear families – A child is a member of two families and parenting is considered a joint venture (joint custody).
- Extended families – A nuclear family plus grandparent(s), cousin(s), aunt(s), and uncle(s) live in one household.
- Same-sex families – Two men or two women live in a common-law or marital arrangement with or without children.
- Commuter families – Adults in the family live and work apart for professional reasons.
- Return-to-nest families – Adult children return home to live for financial, social, or cultural reasons.
- Communal families – A group of people live together with most being unrelated by blood or marriage.
- Foster families – Children are placed temporarily away from their parents in an effort to assure the children's emotional and physical well-being.
- Grandparent-as-parent families – Grandparents raise their child's child(ren) (usually due to the grandparent's child's substance abuse).

Families can be comprised of childless couples, siblings (especially in middle or late life), or a man and woman living together without being married (with or without children), and humans living with companion animals.

FAMILY FUNCTIONS AND ROLES

Adults within families are responsible for their children's growth, development, and behavioral outcomes. Regardless of structure, all families are expected to perform certain tasks. The following functions are universal, but may be influenced by culture. This is what the adults within families ought to do:

- Provide for the physical safety and economic needs of family members by obtaining enough goods, services, and resources to survive.
- Create a sense of family loyalty and an emotionally healthy environment for individual and family well-being.
- Help members develop physically, emotionally, intellectually, and spiritually.
- Foster values based on spiritual and philosophical beliefs, as well as on the cultural and social system that is part of the family identity.
- Teach their children how to effectively communicate their needs, ideas, and feelings.
- Provide social togetherness through the division of labor. With flexibility and cooperation fulfill all roles necessary to the family.
- Socialize the children, teaching values and appropriate behavior, providing adult role models, and fostering positive self-concept and self-esteem.
- Provide relationships and experience within and without the family that foster security, support, encouragement, motivation, morale, and creativity.
- Help members cope with societal demands and crises, and create a place for recuperation from external stressors.
- Maintain authority and decision making, with the parents representing society to the family as a whole, and representing the family unit to society.
- Maintain constructive and responsible ties with school, neighborhood, and broader community.
- Promote integration of each child into society.
- Release family members into the larger society (school, church, work, organizations, government, and eventually, into new families of their own).

Families occasionally have difficulty performing these functions and need assistance from outside resources. A family's ability to perform functions depends on the maturity of the adults and the availability of support systems—health, educational, social, welfare, religious, etc. The adults within most successful families have working philosophies and value systems that are understood and lived. They use healthy and adaptive patterns most of the time. They ask for help and use community resources when needed, developing linkages with nonfamily units and organizations.

Families assign performance roles (breadwinner, homemaker, handyperson, expert, political advisor, chauffer) and emotional roles (leader, nurturer, sustainer, healer, arbitrator, scapegoat, jester, rebel, 'black sheep') to its members. Most members fill multiple roles, and the fewer the members, the more roles any one member must fill. If a member leaves the home, another member or members might need to take on that person's roles. Role accountability refers to family members' sense of responsibility for completing the tasks of their assigned roles. Healthy families create procedures to ensure that necessary family functions are fulfilled. For example, healthy parents understand that they're responsible for disciplining their children. When it's needed, they don't hesitate to discipline because they know that failure to fulfill this role properly will result in child behavior problems, which will disrupt the family's ability to function.

Children learn emotional responses to roles by imitating their parents, experimenting with various roles through play. The more parents pressure children to act in only one certain way, the more likely the child will learn only one role and be uncomfortable with others (athletes may become social misfits, social butterflies might fail school, etc.). These children will also have difficulty with role performance once they form their own families. Healthy families provide ample opportunity for children to exercise various roles, either in actuality or in fantasy.

FUNCTIONAL VERSUS DYSFUNCTIONAL FAMILIES

Family conflict is unavoidable. Families deal with budgets, sibling rivalry, illnesses, insufficient time, lack of shared family responsibilities, and guilt. But conflict need not be viewed as bad or disruptive. When properly managed, conflict leads to change, growth, and improved family functioning. Effective conflict management requires open communication, accurate perceptions of the conflict, and constructive efforts to resolve it. Dysfunctional families have difficulties with one or more of these steps. They trap themselves in patterns that tend to maintain conflict rather than resolve it. Unresolved conflict then adds to the stress that the family needs to cope with.

Stressors, whether from outside or inside the family, contribute to fluctuations in family balance. Some families adapt quickly to extreme crises, while others become chaotic with relatively minor upsets. All families use coping strategies to manage stress, but not all strategies are adaptive (and consequently, successful).

Adaptive coping strategies include the following:
- realizing that stress is temporary and may be positive,
- working together to develop solutions,
- creating new rules that include prioritizing and sharing responsibilities, and
- feeling a sense of accomplishment when dealing with stress.

Maladaptive coping strategies include the following:
- focusing on family problems rather than strengths,
- feeling guilty for allowing stress to exist,
- scapegoating and looking for a place to lay blame rather than finding and working toward a solution to the problem,
- taking sides against each other,
- reducing or withdrawing communications with other family members,
- repetied fighting over the same issues,
- designating one family member as the full-time umpire or problem solver,
- creating only a superficial sense of harmony and togetherness,
- giving in to stress and giving up on trying to cope with it,
- feeling weaker as a family rather than stronger after a common stressful experience,
- growing to dislike family life as a result of accumulating stress, and
- maintaining attitudes that undermine adaptive coping strategies, e.g. "It's not manly to talk about feelings."

Adaptive families achieve equilibrium by talking over problems and finding solutions together. Humor, flexibility, shared work, and leisure help relieve tension. Family members know that certain freedoms exist within their confines that are not available elsewhere. This special feature of a healthy family strengthens each member and the family as a whole.

Many happy, successful people name spouse and family as their most important priority—business or career run second. In a partnership of two such adults, each partner serves as a comforter, listener, companion and counselor to the other. They set aside time to be with each other, sharing uninterrupted time and activity. Such parents often set play dates or other one-to-one time with each of their children.

Even the most stable families might sometimes use ineffective coping mechanisms during times of stress. However, they do not use them often. Are you worried that your family may be teetering on the edge of dysfunction? Here are some signs of strained or destructive family relationships that indicate a need for improvement:

- There is a lack of understanding and helpfulness between family members resulting in conflict and unclear family roles.
- Some family members act as if other members do not exist.
- The family lacks clear decision making and lines of authority.
- An adult within the family is possessive of the children or his partner.
- Children make derogatory remarks toward adults.
- There is extreme closeness between the wife and her family of origin or the husband and his family of origin.
- Parents are domineering with their children.
- There are few outside friends for parents and/or children.
- High levels of anxiety exist within the home.
- There is a lack of stability or creativity.
- A Pattern of immature or regressive behavior exists in either the children or the parents.
- Children carry out parental roles because of a parent's inability or refusal to do so.

PARENTING

Parenting requires a commitment to provide for the needs of a child. It's the most challenging yet rewarding job a person can ever have, and it's one that people sometimes assume with little or no knowledge or experience. For the most part, good parenting tends to be inherited—it is passed down from one generation to the next through example. Unfortunately, bad parenting follows a similar path.

What's your parenting style? Strict? Lenient? Just right? Most parents have a style of parenting that falls somewhere on a continuum of control (exerted by the parent over the child) with authoritarian parents exercising the most control, and uninvolved parents, the least.

Authoritative parents create rigid rules. They expect absolute obedience, without questions from their children about the meaning of the rules. They also expect the children to accept the family's beliefs and principles without explanation. Questioning and disobedience are met with swift and severe punishment that is often physical and accompanied by withdrawal of love and approval. Authoritarian parents come in two types: the authoritarian-directive parent, who is highly intrusive, and the nonauthoritarian-directive parent, who is directive, but not intrusive or oppressive in the use of power. Children of authoritarian parents tend to be shy and withdrawn because they lack self-confidence. They often do well in school, but may lack adequate social skills. Boys of such parents tend to act resistive and hostile.

Authoritative parents show respect for the opinions of their children by allowing them to be different. They develop household rules, but permit discussion if the children do not understand or agree with the rules. Authoritative parents make it clear to the children that parents are the ultimate authority, but discussion and compromise can take place. Their children grow to be happy, independent, and assertive, with high levels of self-esteem.

Permissive or indulgent parents allow considerable self-regulation and avoid confrontation. They tend to be lenient, with little or no control over the behavior of their children. They create rules that are unclear and inconsistent, and they allow their children to decide whether or not they want to follow the rules. If these parents threaten punishment, they may fail to follow through with it. Children of permissive parents tend to be less self-reliant, exhibit little self-control, and often perform less well in school. They may be disobedient, disrespectful, irresponsible, defiant, or aggressive, or They may even take over the parental roles in the household.

Uninvolved parents lack both responsiveness and toughness. In extreme cases, this style may include both rejecting and neglecting behaviors. Children from these families tend to do poorly in all areas of life.

Research shows that parenting is most effective when parents adapt their style to meet the needs of their children at different developmental stages. (The style needed to parent a curious toddler differs greatly from that needed to parent a rebellious teen.)

DADS

In days of old, dads were viewed as wallets (financial support providers), rocks (strict disciplinarians), or Bumsteads (clumsy, but real pals). Current research demonstrates that fathers play an important role in the social, emotional, and intellectual development of their children. A study from Oxford, England that looked at the lives of seventeen thousand children found the following to be true:

- Girls are less likely to have problems later on in life if their fathers are more involved as they grow and mature.
- A strong father/son relationship can prevent boys from getting into trouble with the police.
- A good father/child relationship is associated with greater academic motivation and the absence of emotional and behavioral difficulties in adolescence.
- Teenagers who have grown up feeling close to their fathers also go on to have more satisfactory adult marital relationships.
- A good relationship with the father can protect against adolescent psychological problems in families where the parents have separated.
- Early paternal involvement is usually linked with continued involvement throughout childhood.

These results applied whether or not the father lived with the children, and whether or not the father was the biological father. The key seems to be the level of paternal involvement.

More and more, today's dads are caregivers, combining toughness with tenderness. They want to have a satisfying relationship with their children. However, they're not so different from yesterday's dads when it comes to the division of parenting responsibilities. Fathers still do far less caregiving than mothers, and most dads view their parenting involvement as discretionary.

As a dad, you may well ask, "How can I get more involved?" Well dad, first, you can give each child as much personal attention as possible. Don't allow outside distractions to interfere. Attend school and sports events. Talk, play, read, or learn a skill together with your child. Acknowledge each other and your common interests. Bring your child to work, and let him see what you do there. Some businesses have special days or tours for their employee's children. You can also take your child along when you get the car repaired or go to the hardware store—daughters, too, can appreciate the thrill of power tools. Play ball, go fishing, fly a kite, build models, have a tea party, or surprise mom with breakfast in bed.

Don't be afraid to express your emotions and demonstrate affection. Kiss and hug your child. Provide emotional support, and acknowledge your child as a unique individual. A father who is more affectionate contributes positively to his child's self-esteem.

Get involved with discipline. Good fathers set limits and are firm with their children. Let your child know your beliefs and expectations, but use explanations and reasoning rather than force to confirm your authority.

Value education, regardless of your own educational background. Fathers who respect education have children who do better in school. Start early by reading to your child and fostering her vocabulary. Help with her homework and attend school functions. Get active in the Parent Teach Association/Organization (PTA/PTO). Help your teen decide which college to attend.

The following suggestions and more are included in the US Surgeon General's June 17, 2005 "Tips for fathers and fathers-to-be: Father's Day tips for a healthy childhood" that focuses on father/child interactions with children ages five to nine—the years when many of life's lessons are learned:

- Teach healthy habits for life. Encourage at least sixty minutes of physical activity every day. Limit television, video games, and computer time. Teach your child to wash her hands properly. Talk with her about avoiding alcohol, tobacco, drugs, and inhalants. Be a good role model for all these healthy habits. Don't smoke, and don't let anyone else to smoke around your child. (If you need help to quit smoking, call 1-800-QUIT-NOW (1-800-784-8669) or visit www.Smokefree.gov today.)
- Always use an appropriate car safety seat, installed properly in the back seat of the car. Children should ride in a safety seat with a harness until they ougrow it. Then they should ride in a belt-positioning booster seat until at least age eight. You can tell when your child is ready for a booster seat (when she reaches the top weight or height allowed for the safety seat)—her shoulders will be above the harness slots, or her ears will have reached the top of the safety seat. If you have any questions about safety or booster seats, contact your local fire or police department. Once your child has outgrown a booster seat, be sure that she always wears a

seatbelt in your car or any vehicle she rides in. There is more information on this at (www.cdc.gov)

- Practice prevention and safety. Teach your child about staying safe. This includes teaching the following rules: always swim under adult supervision; use safety equipment that can reduce injuries; and always wear helmets and protective gear when bicycling, playing contact sports, using in-line skates, or riding a skateboard. (Supervise children ages five to nine when crossing busy streets.) Teach your child about sun safety, including wearing a hat outdoors and frequently applying SPF 30 sunscreen. If you own a firearm, remove it from your home, or keep it unloaded and locked up. Store all ammunition separately from all firearms. Be sure your child knows his own name, parents' names, and phone number(s). Help him to recognize police and fire officials as trusted individuals, while raising healthy caution about other strangers. Get his fingerprints taken and keep recent photographs in your wallet. (See more at www.healthfinder.gov)

- Teach and practice healthy eating. Provide three nutritious meals a day, supplemented with two healthy snacks. Share meals as a family. Avoid foods and drinks that are high in sugar or caffeine. Be a good role model and follow the Dietary Guidelines for Americans. (See these at www.healthierus.gov)

- Encourage good oral health. Cavities are the second-most common chronic childhood disease in the United States. Supervise your child's toothbrushing twice a day with a soft toothbrush. Teach her to floss and brush her teeth without supervision when she reaches the age of eight. Talk with your dentist about fluoride and dental sealants, and make sure your child has regular dental appointments. Learn dental emergency care. (See more at www.nidcr.nih.gov)

- Practice positive parenting. Show affection for your child and recognize his accomplishments. Encourage him to express his feelings. Read interactively with him. As he learns to read, listen as he reads out loud to you. Teach family rules, set limits, establish consequences, and assign responsibilities. Help your child set achievable goals so that he learns the important skill of taking pride in himself and relying less on approval or rewards from others. Talk with your child about school, friends, and things he looks forward to in the future. Talk with him about respecting others, and encourage him to help people in need. Expect curiosity and be prepared to answer his questions about his body. Explain that certain body parts are private. Do fun things together as a family, such as playing games, reading, and going to events in your community. (See more on this at www.cdc.gov)

- Maximize school success. Meet with teachers and prepare your child to enter school positively, for the first year of school and every year thereafter. Talk about new opportunities, friends, and activities at school. Tour the school with your child, and get involved in school activities. If your child has trouble concentrating or is hyperactive, talk to your healthcare professional. Your child could have attention-deficit / hyperactivity disorder (ADHD), one of the most common childhood behavioral disorders, which can persist into adulthood. Symptoms begin before age seven and can cause serious difficulties in home, school, or work life. However, ADHD can be managed through behavioral and/or medical interventions. (Find out more at www.cdc.gov)
- Fully immunize your child on time. Immunizations prevent death and disease for millions of children. (Find out more about this at www.cdc.gov)
- Prevent violence. Prevent bullying by demonstrating peaceful resolutions to conflict and by teaching your child to build positive relationships. Encourage respect for others and their differences. Limit your child's exposure to violence in the media, in the community, and at home. A child who grows up in a family environment filled with violence may learn to view violence as normal, acceptable behavior. Teach your child that there is no place for verbal or physical violence by setting an example with your words and actions. (Learn more at www.stopbullyingnow.hrsa.gov)
- Pay attention to important milestones. For example, a child at ages six to eight years should be able to dress herself, catch a ball more easily with only her hands, and tie her shoes. She should also show more independence from parents and family, a stronger sense of right and wrong, a growing desire to be liked and accepted by friends, and a greater ability to describe experiences and talk about thoughts and feelings. If you have concerns, talk with her school or a healthcare professional to decide if developmental screening is warranted. (Learn more about developmental milestones at www.cdc.gov)
- Learn CPR and child first aid. Know how to call for help, including poison control (1-800-222-1222). Make sure your child knows

basic first aid and other age-appropriate ways to help in an emergency, including dialing 911. Keep these important numbers stored in your phone and listed by your phone. (Learn more at www.nlm.nih.gov)

- Make sure your child has a primary health provider, such as a pediatrician, family doctor, or nurse practitioner. (Get more information at www.ahrq.gov or at www.napnap.org)

Dad is critically important to the proper growth and development of his children. If a father is absent, mother has the responsibility to assure that her child has a responsible and caring adult male role model. If there is absolutely no positive male role model, contact a mentoring organization such as Big Brothers/Big Sisters. (Learn more at www.bbbsa.org)

GRANDPARENTS

The more love kids get, the better they thrive, and grandparents frequently have the opportunity to spend more relaxed time with children. Dr. Arthur Kornhaber, author of *The Grandparent Guide*, states that the unconditional love of grandparents is second only in emotional power to the parent/child bond. The relationship may even be stronger if the parents are, busy professionals, travel extensively, or are separated, divorced, or just neglectful. Grandparents are more effective with and necessary for children than are preschools, daycares, or a room full of child specialists.

Grandparents may play many roles in a child's life. They act as oral historians, teaching about family history, the child's roots, the meanings of pictures and objects, and the "good old days." They're great mentors, showing children how to create, mend and fix things. And they provide spiritual sustenance when parents are busy or indifferent.

Studies show that a child who has strong relationships with her grandparents develops a good sense of family and security. She will do better in school and feel more comfortable in relationships. She will also tend to abstain from drugs and violence.

Sadly a growing number of grandparents lose contact with their grandchildren due to parental divorce, parental conflict, death of adult children, and adoption of grandchildren after remarriage. Many of these parents seek legal means to ensure visitation rights or to gain custody. If grandparents are deceased or unavailable, adopt one!

Nursing homes and assisted living facilities are full of older people with lots of love to give—and your child may help one of them live a fuller, more rewarding life.

FAMILY TIME

Family time is a most precious time for both children and parents. Let your children spend it with you now. Listen to the late Harry Chapin's song, "Cat's in the Cradle" (http://www.harrychapin.com/music/cats.shtml), and don't let that be you. Don't let family time be a vague memory to your children as they age. Be a family becoming a better family. Take lots of family photos and display them all over your house and office. Include pictures of intergenerational relationships at family gatherings.

Children flourish when they are part of a large, loving family. Have family get-togethers with extended family members, grandparents, and other relatives. Make holidays and birthdays extended family events. Wear special outfits. Create traditions for these occasions. Allow the birthday person to choose the menu or sit at the head of the table. Color Easter eggs with grandpa. Make Christmas ornaments with grandma. Bake red-white-and-blue cupcakes for July Fourth with Uncle Sam. Decorate the hall for cousin Jonathan's Bar Mitzvah. Your children will carry on these traditions when they have families of their own.

5

UNIQUENESS

Uniqueness is what makes a person an individual and allows her to express herself in her own way. So why, then would we treat children as if they're all the same? As each snowflake is unique, so is each child. It is our job to recognize, celebrate, and protect her uniqueness.

*****

The kids next door, William, Oliver, Olivia, Molly, Noah, and Harley aside from their ages and sizes, look almost identical. Yet they are quite different. William explores the adventures of his own backyard, while Oliver prefers to play video games indoors. Olivia has become quite the horsewoman, and Molly's as comfortable playing rough-and-tumble as she is playing with her Barbies. No one knows trucks like Noah, and little Harley's just finding his way in the world.

Self-perception has a pervasive effect on all aspects of life, and a child's self-concept consists of a collection of attitudes what he thinks, believes, and feels about himself. These attitudes form a personal belief system he refers to as "me". When parents have little time to focus on their child's uniqueness, and when schools pressure him to strive for success only in those areas that can be measured, he can lose his sense of individuality. As noted by Kimberly L. Keith's *Guide to*

Parenting of K-6 Children, to be truly unique, a child needs to do the following things:

- know that there is something special about himself,
- know and do things that others can't,
- express himself in his own voice,
- use his imagination and creativity,
- respect himself, and
- take pleasure in being different

INDIVIDUALS FROM THE BEGINNING

Children are born with their personalities (and chances are, your kids get the personalities your parents wished on you when you were growing up). Each infant shows a distinct pattern of reaction from birth—calm and cuddly, alert and active, or cranky and resistant. Her underlying style stays pretty much the same as she grows, but she demonstrates it in different ways during different life stages. The calm and cuddly child moves slowly from mom, gradually becoming interested in her environment; the alert and active one toddles off eager to explore; the cranky and resistant one wants to do what she wants when she wants to do it. Busy kids grow into energetic teens who turn out to be adults on the go. Second children are rarely like their older siblings, and even identical twins have differences.

Each child has her own ways of walking, talking, writing, and tossing a ball. Each is different from the next in her abilities use language, add, subtract, multiply, and spell. Each sees, hears, tastes, smells and feels in a different way. The variety is infinite, and each child deserves to be treated as a unique individual in order for her to develop a healthy self-concept.

A person with a healthy self-concept exhibits a clear sense of self and others. He knows who he is in the world, and he can distinguish himself as a separate individual with strengths and weaknesses. He acknowledges his emotions and finds productive ways to bring meaning to life. He views others realistically and is able to relate to them in a satisfying manner. He has the capacity for intimacy and love. He can handle life's realities and problems with appropriate coping behaviors.

One's self image consists of body image, self-esteem, personal identity and role performance. But a child's self-image, his uniqueness, is more than just the sum of these parts.

Body Image denotes the way a person sees and feels about her body. It is the unifying concept behind the way she feels about her size, sex, and sexuality, the way she looks, the way her body functions, and whether her body is helping her accomplish her goals.

Self-Esteem refers to the way a person feels about himself. High self-esteem develops through parental acceptance, clear expectations, limitations, and the freedom to express opinions. From these four childhood experiences, he develops power (the sense that his opinions count and will be heard), meaning (the sense of being valued and worthwhile), competence (personal success), and virtue (adherence to a moral or ethical standard).

Personal Identity stands for an organized principle of the self—that a person is distinctly separate from others. A strong identity provides a person with a sense of continuity through time.

Role Performance denotes how a person performs overall in the many roles he assumes.

Individuality underlies child's self-perception and self-concept, his sense of personal identity, goals, emotional patterns, and feelings bout himself. The significance of his sense of self is best exemplified by his personal experiences. When a child feels good about himself, he shows it in the positive way he looks and acts. Conversely, when he feels unable to accomplish anything worthwhile, a child shows it with negative behaviors and changes in his eating, sleeping and activity patterns.

Self-concept grows throughout each stage of the lifespan, starting with infancy:

- A newborn can't differentiate herself from another. However, parents transmit their own self-concepts, as well as their anxieties. When parents act calmly, they help their newborn establish the basis for a healthy self-concept. Research confirms that an infant has the ability to form a self-concept—a four-month-old is fascinated with her mirror image, more so than by a photo of another infant. As she grows, many factors, including her relationship with her parents combine to help her form her self-concept.
- A toddler's developing intellectual, language, and motor skills provide his means for building his self-concept. He discovers that his behavior is his own, and that it has an effect on others. He can separate from others by walking away and may choose not to cooperate when he's told to do something. He must explore the world to develop a true sense of independence. Exploring his physical world involves poking, climbing, crawling, chewing and taking apart

nearly everything in reach. Exploring his interpersonal world means searching for the limits of his power within relationships by saying no and having temper tantrums. Discipline is a must, but parents should discipline in a manner that preserves his uniqueness.

- A preschooler continues to develop and refine her sense of self through task-oriented and socially oriented experiences. Self-esteem is developed through the reinforcement of her skills and capabilities. She also uses her rich imagination to try out roles. Pretending to be her parents (or babysitters) allows her to imagine and act out the feelings of others, a safe way for her to experiment with new ideas and feelings.

- A school-age child engages in self-discovery through his expanding physical, intellectual, and social development. Through these growing abilities, he builds his own personality, increase his ability to relate to others, and becomes exposed to a wide range of possibilities for his own attitudes, values, and behaviors. With greater intellectual abilities, he can better understand the identifying traits of himself and others, such as race, gender, and disability. He can compare himself to his peers, measuring looks, abilities, and social influence. This experience can have either positive or negative results. This is the time when he learns that it can be painful to be different. Uniqueness has it's price among peers. So parents need to be extremely supportive of their school-age child's self-esteem and self-concept, all the way through adolescence.

- An adolescents experiences incredible changes as her body matures, and these changes affect her self-concept. If she perceives her body as being less desirable than those of her peers she may develop less favorable feelings about herself and a poorer self-concept. Peers and role models (sports figures and other celebrities) can strongly influence her self-concept. This may result in her choosing particular hair and clothing styles, and behaving in certain ways. These become part of her adolescent rebellion, a way for her to develop and define her personal identity and uniqueness.

SELF-ESTEEM

A child's self-esteem can be his shield against the cruelties of the world. It helps him feel proud of his accomplishments and abilities, and it gives him the courage to try new things. The more positive your child's self-esteem, the more successful he'll be at dealing with life. Self-esteem gives your child the power to believe in himself, and to respect himself, even when he makes mistakes. And when he respects himself, others will be more likely to respect him, too.

A child with healthy self-esteem feels that her parents love her, accept her, and would do anything to ensure her safety and well-being. She tends to have an easier time handling conflicts and resisting negative pressures. She tends to exhibit some or all of the following traits:

- She is happy with herself the way she is.
- She is assertive and confident, but not arrogant.
- She is able to handle criticism and not be harshly critical of herself.
- She has intrinsic motivation toward achievement.
- She is not easily defeated by setbacks.
- She is able to learn from her mistakes.
- She is self-reliant, but is able to ask for help when she needs it.
- She is unlikely to put others down.
- She is not worried about failing or looking silly.
- She is able to laugh at herself.

Occasional bouts of low self-esteem are common as a child masters new skills or sets new goals. But a child with chronic poor self-esteem typically has difficulty finding appropriate solutions to problems. He either feels down on himself, or he feels angry and wants to get even. He is likely to exhibit some or all of the following traits:

- He is overwhelmed by life and feels like a failure.
- He is overly dependent, timid and not assertive.
- He doesn't put effort into things because he believes he will fail anyway.
- He puts himself down.
- He loses his temper, picks fights, blames others and constantly finds fault with things.
- He is negative, constantly argues, and takes pleasure in others' troubles.

Put simply, self-esteem is a measurement of how much a child values herself and how important she thinks she is. Self-esteem is how she feels about herself and her accomplishments. It is her personal judgment of her worthiness derived from and influenced by social groups in the immediate environment and her own perceptions of how she is valued by others. Thus, high self-esteem is primarily a function of being loved and gaining the respect of others.

Self-esteem begins at birth and develops throughout life. It is influenced by parental love, effective relationships with friends and others, success in school, play and other activities, and gaining skills and self-control in the activities of daily living. Thus the seeds of self-esteem are both internal and external. The internal seeds come from child's own pleasure at having accomplished tasks such as walking, hitting a homer, or making the honor roll. When he achieves his goals, he is delighted, fueling his self-confidence. Every child needs to believe that he is good at something, and that he is a unique individual.

The external seeds come from parents when they tell him that they love him and when they recognize his accomplishments with enthusiasm. For a child to fully understand that he has succeeded, he needs the approval of others, as well as of himself. He needs to know that he did a good job by hearing his parents verbalize it. Approval from other adults, such as teachers and group leaders, is also important, as are tangible validations, such as badges, stars, or privileges. But these pale when compared to approval from his parents.

Once a child reaches the school years, the peer group's influence on her self-esteem is unquestionable. Her self-esteem blossoms with a sense of belonging and acceptance from her peers. The resulting success or failure during competition with peers helps to develop her sense of adequacy.

BUILDING CHILDREN'S SELF-ESTEEM

The more positive your own self-esteem, the more positive your child's self-esteem will be. If you are overly critical of yourself, pessimistic, or unrealistic about your abilities and limitations, your child will learn to imitate you and will do likewise. Parents with high self-esteem usually have a strong parent-to-parent relationship, and they are affectionate, supportive, and firm in setting behavioral guidelines.

Understand and accept yourself, acknowledge your strengths and accept and celebrate your personal uniqueness. Take care of yourself, treat yourself with respect, and be aware of your own feelings. Boost your own self-esteem, and be a good role model. Every time you think negatively about yourself, counteract it with a personal affirmation. Remember that there are things about yourself that you can't change.

Learn to accept them, and to love them. Appreciate your body as your own, no matter what size, shape, or color it comes in.

Give your child unconditional love. Get to know him. See what he sees, feel what he feels, and hope what he hopes. Each has his own strengths, dreams, and opinions, and each needs to be loved, accepted, and respected for who he is. Be there for him to reinforce the importance of his efforts.

Value your child. Accept and praise her for who she is and not just for what she does Demonstrate your belief in her ability to improve and grow. Unconditional love means that you accept her even when she does something undesirable. When she does misbehave, disapprove of the behavior, not your child.

Identify his strengths, focus on his efforts, and offer thanks for what he does for you. Avoid criticism, shame and humiliation. Unconditional love means letting go. Develop a gradual plan to grant freedom and responsibility, beginning in infancy and ending in late adolescence. Offer trust, provide opportunities, give choices, instill confidence, and refrain from rushing to his aid when he can learn to help himself.

CREATE A SAFE, NURTURING HOME ENVIRONMENT

Protect and respect your child, and make your home a safe haven. Don't tolerate violent behavior or abusive language in any form. Avoid constant arguing and fighting between you and your spouse, as it can cause depression and withdrawal in your child (and it is not what you want to model for him). Instead, foster positive problem solving. Watch for signs of problems in school, trouble with peers, abuse by others, or anything that may negatively affect his self-esteem.

Express verbal and physical affection, especially when your child is physically or emotionally injured. Acknowledge his right to have his own feelings, friends, opinions, and activities. Participate in his life (school, sports, special events), and include him in your activities. Be gentle and kind, and maintain a family routine. Talk and act so that he feels safe and comfortable expressing himself.

AVOID COMPARISONS

Don't measure your child against other children, no matter how eager you are for her to succeed. This destroys uniqueness and may cause her to feel that she must be competitive with others to gain your attention and approval. No two children are alike, no matter how you raise them, not even identical twins. Respect her uniqueness and abilities, and praise her for these assets.

USE OPEN, TWO-WAY COMMUNICATION

Talk *with* your child, not *at* him. That means listening to how he feels without being judgmental. Listening means paying full attention—without interference from other family members, the television, radio, computer, or other intrusions. Take him seriously, be interested in what he has to say, and let him finish talking before you speak.

Be conscious of the words you use, your tone of voice, the impact of your words, and your body language. Avoid negative messages—labeling, humiliating, and finding fault. He is likely to believe these negative messages, no matter how harmless they may appear to you.

Here is a mild warning: Continuously complimenting your child can create anxiety—if she feels she must live up to what she hears as high expectations.

To avoid this pifall, give honest praise. Focus on her positive behavior and praise it. Honest praise is the fastest way to build her self-esteem. Praise her frequently without overdoing it, and make sure the praise is realistic and honest. Your child can tell when something's coming from the heart and when it's not. Not only will false praise do nothing to boost her self-esteem, it will most likely put a strain on her trust in your relationship.

ENCOURAGE, BUT DON'T PRESSURE YOUR CHILD

He needs encouragement at all levels of development, and you can provide it both verbally and nonverbally. Encourage him to develop at his own rate. Don't force him into activities before he's ready and willing. Instead, encourage him to explore and occasionally take reasonable risks. Accept and even expect mistakes under these circumstances, and treat mistakes as learning experiences. Pressuring him toward perfection can be detrimental. It discourages normal, healthy development, and can interfere with his participation in activities—he won't want to try new things for fear he won't succeed.

REDIRECT YOUR CHILD'S INACCURATE BELIEFS

She may sometimes have unfounded beliefs about herself, particularly about her attractiveness, perfection, and abilities. These misperceptions can take root and seem real to her especially when they're reinforced by the media, overripe with distorted images. Encourage her to examine each inaccurate belief, then help her adjust her thinking on the matter. Point out how well she does in other areas and help her find ways to improve in any area she's struggling with.

HELP YOUR CHILDREN SET REALISTIC GOALS

Dreams can seem far off, too difficult, and even completely unreachable. To make dreams come true, your child can build pathways to them by identifying the goals he needs to achieve. However, the easiest way to fail is to aim for impossible goals. If he sets unrealistic goals, the chance for success diminishes, along with his self-esteem. Instead, assist him in developing realistic, developmentally appropriate goals.

Goals can be feats that people strive to accomplish. They can be as concrete as getting a B in math, or as abstract as getting better at controlling one's temper. When your child sets goals and works to achieve them, she engages her intelligence, abilities, time, and energy. Setting goals helps her define how she wants to live and what she wants to achieve—from major life decisions to the simplest day-to-day activities.

GET YOUR CHILD INVOLVED IN CONSTRUCTIVE ACTIVITIES

He needs to feel successful at some task, especially once he reaches the school-age years. He has particular interests, and abilities that can be developed and displayed to provide him with a sense of success and a defense against failure. Find out what he is in and good at, then encourage and praise him in developing those interests and talents.

Your child has many opportunities for success through school, organizational sports, and after-school activities. But these structured activities might not match his interests or talents. Encourage him to be resourceful in finding ways to pursue the activities develop the talents in order to nurture his self-esteem and sense of uniqueness.

Set high standards for your child but don't overestimate her abilities. Be aware of what she can and can't do. Encourage her to continue to excel in areas that she already excels in, and support her in areas where she needs improvement. Provide opportunities that allow her to succeed, and help her to help herself.

HELP YOUR CHILD TO DO WELL IN SCHOOL

Poor academic performance is both a cause and an effect of low self-esteem; along with a low commitment to school, it's a risk factor for other negative behaviors. Help your child do well in school, and show her that you are committed to their education. Don't do her homework for her. Instead, provide assistance and suggestions when asked, and praise her best efforts.

Healthy self-esteem is a cornerstone of a happy childhood. Help shape it by fostering your child's uniqueness.

6

HEROES

Everyone needs a hero now and then. Kids just need them more often. They need heroes to show them how to behave during tough situations, to inspire them to see beyond times of struggle or disappointment, and to serve as guides to solving problems and helping others. They need true heroes who sacrifice for the benefit of others, not celebrities who thrive on others benefiting them. Heroes live in books, on the big screen, in ball parks, in the community, and right in the living room. They can be as super as Spiderman, as athletic as Michael Jordan, as furry as Fido, or as regular as mom and dad. Without them a child's world is a pretty bleak place. Children have an essential need for heroes.

*****

To get the scoop on childhood heroes, I asked my nephew Christopher, age 10, and my nieces, Gianna and Daniella, ages eight and four, respectively, to name their heroes. Chris jumped right in with Navy Seals, the Army, and the Air Force for his real-life heroes, and Toby McGuire and Arnold Schwarzenegger as the actor counterparts of his fictional heroes. The latter were interesting intergenerational choices, since the young McGuire appeals to oldsters like me, and 80's idol

Schwarzenegger still has the right stuff for today's kids. Gianna claimed her parents as her main heroes, followed by the police, fire fighters, and her teachers. Hillary Duff as Lizzy McGuire reigned as her fictional hero. But chatty little Daniella had the longest list. Starting with "grandma and grandpa," she immediately rattled off the names of most of her family, including aunts and uncles. She then added construction workers, firemen, ambulance drivers, Jimmy Neutron, dogs, and elephants. I understood dogs, but not elephants, until she explained that elephants "get water from their trunks to put out fires." I was thrilled to see that heroism is alive and well in my family.

HEROISM AND CELEBRITY

Heroes have been around since the beginning of mankind, honored in ancient cave paintings and in folklore and myth. Societies transmitted stories of heroism through legends, folktales, and myths, both spoken and written. Modern societies maintain the tradition of honoring heroes not only in literary works but also in film and television.

Heroism has been traditionally defined as self-risk in the service of the physical well-being of others, or in terms of courage and risk of one's life as well, as nobility of purpose. But these definitions don't clearly indicate that it is the conjunction of risk-taking and service to a socially valued goal that yields heroic status. Actions that have both of these attributes are far more likely to yield heroic status than actions that have only one. Therefore, people who take risks merely for pleasure or to attract attention, as in extreme sports, are not deemed heroic, nor are people who serve valued social goals without risk to their own life or health, as in community volunteering. Consistent with this definition, actions recognized as heroic are ordinarily performed voluntarily, and thus do not include police, firefighters, and the military. By requiring risk to one's life and by excluding work-related deeds, this limited definition would bar persons, such as Mother Theresa and the professionals involved in 9/11, from being called heroes.

Heroism is much more than celebrity. We've become much too accustomed to a plethora of superlatives used to describe actors, models, and sports figures who do no more than entertain. Yes, some do great things, but far too many have a knack for doing those "great things" just as their latest movie premieres. Valiant acts done in the name of publicity are not heroic. True heroes ask nothing of us, nor do they seek fame and fortune. Celebrities, on the other hand, are famous simply by definition, and usually use that fame, by their own design or that of others, to elicit sales—books, DVDs, tickets, etc. But heroes and celebrities occasionally blur into one. Some celebrities are extremely generous with their time—the late Christopher Reeve and, Rosie O'Donnell, the late Elizabeth Glasser, Sting, Bono, and Susan Sarandon, to name a few. And some fictitious heroes gain celebrity—Spiderman, Batman, Indiana Jones.

True heroism exists in those who sacrifice themselves in some manner to perform acts of greatness that benefit others. Their sacrifices can range from donating their time to forfeiting their lives, while acts of greatness run the continuum from helping someone learn to read to expanding and defending civil rights. True heroes are complex. They make mistakes and do things they regret, but they learn from them and move on. True heroes overcome tremendous odds and reach down inside themselves to find the inner strength to succeed. In other words, true heroism is the whole of one's life, not just a single event.

Unfortunately, today's children see too much celebrity and too little heroism. They're blitzed with media images of near-naked pop tarts and substance-abusing sports figures, as well as the movie-heroes-of-the-moment, whose faces adorn posters, clothing, and merchandise until the next illusionary hero comes along. Celeb exposure can be a good thing, provided that they're positive role models and not the only role models that children are exposed to. Children need to believe that they can accomplish things, just like real-life heroes, and that they, too, can make mistakes, learn from them, keep striving, and eventually succeed.

KIDS AND REAL LIFE HEROES

Like almost everything else in childhood, choices of heroes tend to follow predictable patterns based on a child's level of development. A young child frequently chooses his parents or teachers because he sees these immediate caregivers as having the greatest moral authority. As children grow, they begin to see peers as heroes, usually someone who has attained a level of celebrity as a rock star or sports figure. Older teens value people who think for themselves.

Children need to know that there are real heroes in the world—heroes who do not wear tights, spin webs, or blast things to smithereens. As they make their way through life and encounter morally complex situations, children may have a difficult time figuring out right from wrong. When they have a hero to admire and respect, they can reason out a situation by thinking: "What would [my hero] do in this situation?" It is tough teaching children about complex values such as honesty, civility, courage, perseverance, loyalty, self-restraint, compassion, tolerance and responsibility, but having a hero who has these qualities makes learning them much easier.

Kids see in heroes what they want to see in themselves—the ability to overcome fear, weakness, and insecurity, and to be brave and courageous. By showing our children real, everyday heroes, children realize that they too, as ordinary people, can have heroic attributes, and that they can nurture their budding feelings of courage or compassion. Children tend to grow to be like the people they admire. To help your children find appropriate heroes, consider the following suggestions:

- Expose your child to people who do heroic things, such as firefighters, police, and nurses. (Let preschoolers play dress-up with cool symbols—badges, helmets, uniforms, and nurse kits.)
- Talk about your personal heroes, those you admire now, as well as those you looked up to when you were a child. It's a great way to share dreams and aspirations.
- Don't pass judgment on your child's heroes. Instead, try to find their positive attributes and focus on those.
- Praise your child for doing heroic things, such as sticking up for a friend who was bullied.
- Encourage your child to read about real life heroes. Research them on the Internet, read their biographies, or have your child write her own stories about her favorite heroes.

Here's a list with some examples:

HERO LIST

(Just a sample of heroes for you and your child to research and learn about)

Amelia Earhart	Lewis and Clark
Jane Addams	Robert E. Lee
Maya Angelou	John Lennon
Susan B. Anthony	Abraham Lincoln
Clara Barton	Yo Yo Ma
Elizabeth Blackwell	George Marshall
Ruby Bridges	Mother Teresa

Rachel Carson	Rita Moreno
Jimmy Carter	John Muir
George Washington Carver	Sandra Day O'Connor
Mary Cassatt	Jesse Owens
Cesar Chavez and Dolores Huerta	Rosa Parks
Roberto Clemente	I.M. Pei
Bill Cosby	Christopher Reeve
Walt Disney	Cal Ripken, Jr.
Frederick Douglass	Jackie Robinson and Branch Rickey
Thomas Edison	Roy Rogers and Dale Evans
Albert Einstein	Eleanor Roosevelt
Anne Frank	Franklin D. Roosevelt
Benjamin Franklin	Sacajawea
Elizabeth Glasser	Jonas Salk
John Glenn	Albert Schweitzer
Martha Graham	Anne Sullivan
Matthew Henson	Tecumseh
Milton Hershey	Harry Truman
Langston Hughes	Harriet Tubman
Thomas Jefferson	George Washington
Raul Julia	Elie Weisel
Helen Keller	Ida B. Wells
Quincy Jones	Oprah Winfrey
Jackie Joyner-Kersee	Wilbur and Orville Wright
Martin Luther King, Jr.	Malcolm X

Suggested reading: *50 American Heroes Every Kid Should Meet* by Dennis Denenberg and Lorraine Roscoe (The Millbrook Press, 2001).

KIDS AND FICTIONAL HEROES

Real life heroes are a must for children. However, they pose two major problems: 1) they seem too fallible to fight the monsters in our closets, and, 2) they're not always around when you need them. So, enter the not-so-real heroes, the ones who populate fables, books, movies, comics, and cartoons. There's one to conquer any and all evils, and they're there with the flip of a page, the click of a button, or the magic of the imagination.

Fictional heroes come in two types—superheroes and everyday heroes. Superheroes include Superman, Batman, Wonder Woman, and Spiderman. Spiderman has a wide range of fans, partly due to his superhuman powers, but mostly because of his vulnerability and mistakes, which give him human qualities that children can identify with. Superheroes are fun to imitate, but everyday heroes—Kevin McAllister, Shrek, Ariel, Simba, Belle, Dorothy, Luke Skywalker, and Mulan—make a bigger impact on young and older minds alike, especially when they fit into the "Hollywood Hero Formula." The hero:

- does something that kids can relate to (usually the hero's flaw);
- suffers a huge loss that sends him off on his journey;
- finds a mentor to guide him along the way;
- faces trials and tribulations;
- narrowly escapes death, usually a few times;
- overcomes his flaw and defeats the bad guy; and
- celebrates with those who shared his journey.

This formula works so well that it is highly touted in screenwriting and filmmaking books and seminars—(and it makes billions on merchandizing). Most importantly, it let's kids be heroes vicariously, learning valuable life lessons along the way. Using Kevin McAllister from *Home Alone* as an example, here's the formula:

- Everyone picks on Kevin, who feels totally incompetent—something most kids his age easily relate to.
- Angry for being punished, somewhat unjustly, Kevin wishes his family would disappear. When he wakes up, they're gone. The house is targeted by burglars.
- He befriends the old man next door.
- Kevin uses techniques only a child could think of to defend his home from the thieves.
- He narrowly escapes a few times. When Kevin is caught by the thieves, the old man comes to his rescue.
- The thieves are captured by the police. Kevin discovers he's not so incompetent after all, and realizes how much he misses his family.
- The family returns for a big reunion, and Kevin shares a warm moment with the old man, whom Kevin helped reunite with his family.

Kevin is an ordinary kid who overcomes his fears to do extraordinary things. What a great hero!

PARENTS AS HEROES

It's Supermom and Superdad to the rescue! Scary thought, isn't it? Parents are not perfect, but neither are the best heroes. It's the hero's ability to overcome adversity that attracts us. So, as "flawed" as you think you are, you still are your child's most important heroes. They learn by watching you, even when you don't realize it. You act as their key source of guidance and encouragement, and by design or default, you are sustaining models of the adult world and adaptation to life—everyday heroes.

Children watch and listen as their parents go about their day. They notice whether you drink too much or not at all, if you speed down the road or obey traffic rules, whether you argue a lot or very little, and if you solve problems by discharging anger or by using problem-solving methods. They observe your selfishness or generosity, and they learn how male and female adults act.

Why do your children imitate your behavior? Imitation allows them to learn about social activity, adult roles, and cultural norms. By behaving like you, they gain and maintain your affection and avoid punishment. They also acquire a sense of mastery over their environment by imitating the behavior of warm, competent, and powerful parents.

Parents cannot expect children to engage in positive behaviors simply because they tell them to do so, while the parents, themselves, engage in inappropriate behaviors. If your children notice that you go to church regularly and hear you talk about how moral you are, yet also observe you cheating on your taxes, ignoring traffic rules, exhibiting road rage, and treating others with little respect, they will more often imitate your actions than follow your words. Actions really do speak louder than words.

Here are some ways you can be a hero in your child's eyes:

- Show your love for family members. Let them know that you look forward to spending time with them, then spend time with them. Make plans ahead of time and do something special, like go to the movies or a sports event. Have at least one meal together every day, and share your daily experiences. Hold family game nights. Enjoy spur of the moment activities like going out for ice cream or building a snowman. Don't forget lots of hugs and kisses. Say, "I love you."
- Display positive interaction with your spouse. Marital conflict happens. Handle it with care. When disagreements erupt, calmly

discuss your differences. Show your children that you can work out disputes without aggression. Use your problem-solving skills to come up with a mutual agreement. Whatever you do, don't argue in front of your kids.

- Share your values and live by them. Your children won't know the family values unless you discuss them. Talk about important values such as honesty, respect, and responsibility, and address your values on alcohol and other drug use. Remember, talk is cheap. If you want your children to develop your values, you must live them yourself.

- Demonstrate your own self-esteem and respect. Take good care of yourself. Eat right, exercise, take pride in your accomplishments. Feel good about yourself, and let it show. Your children's positive self-esteem starts with yours, so provide them with valuable behaviors that they can imitate.

- Show that you value independence—heroes stand on their own two feet. By both your words and your actions, let your children know that you value independence. Show them that you prefer to make your own decisions, and that you don't need to follow the crowd. Don't keep up with the Joneses. Just because your neighbors forfeit family time to make those extra dollars to get a bigger and better car doesn't mean that you have to. Show your children that you don't need to do what everyone one does, and that you value family time more than material possessions.

- Handle stress well. When you have minor stressors, talk them over with your children, and let them see how you manage them. Show them that you can deal with stress successfully by using positive measures such as problem-solving and relaxation techniques. Help them see that you view stress as a necessary part of life to promote growth and change. However, avoid discussing significant stressors, such as martial or financial problems, as these are inappropriate for children to worry about.

- Share your successes and failures. Heroes typically fail several times before they finally succeed. When making an attempt to change your own behavior, such as quitting smoking, or applying for a promotion, talk about it openly with your children. Let them share your success, but also let them know about your failures and how you manage to rebound from them. This will help them know that it's okay to make mistakes, and that mistakes can be meaningful. Change isn't easy, and mistakes create opportunities to learn.

They'll learn how to handle mistakes with dignity, how to accept responsibility for their mistakes, and how to move on and not let the mistakes hold them back from growing.

- Get involved with your community. Show your children that true heroes help others in their time of need. Volunteer. Spend a few hours each week helping out at your place of worship, the local soup kitchen or animal shelter, the library, or any other place in need of volunteers. Bring your children with you so that they can see what you do.
- Make a difference and leave your mark on the world. If you raise great kids, they become your legacy, and you've made a huge difference.

KIDS AS HEROES

Iqbal Masih was sold into slavery at age four by his father. For over six years, a factory owner forced Iqbal to work more than twelve hours a day in a carpet factory in Pakistan. He was beaten, verbally abused and chained to his station. Finally, freed by a human rights group, he became a human right's activist, speaking out against child slavery, encouraging others to speak out, and freeing many children. Iqbal came to the United States in 1994, but was murdered on his return home at age twelve. At the time of his death, his dream was to become a lawyer to continue his fight to free Pakistan's seven and a half million illegally enslaved children.

Few humans reach the heroic level of Iqbal. Yet we read about the heroic deeds of children on a regular basis—campaigning against carnivals to end animal cruelty, rescuing families from fires, and administering CPR at ages as young as four. Most of us have read the *Diary of Ann Frank* or heard how bravely Ruby Bridges attended first grade as the first African-American to desegregate an elementary school in New Orleans.

Every child has hero potential. To cultivate heroism, try these suggestions by Wendy Lawton:

- Encourage your child's their relationship with God. Faith is a critical component of heroism.
- Raise child with a sense of community, so that he understands the need to help others.
- Encourage her to take initiative. Heroes sometimes have to act with split-second timing.

MYHERO.COM

MYHERO.com is a not-for-profit educational web project that celebrates the best of humanity. Their mission is to inform and inspire people of all ages with an ever-growing archive of hero stories from around the world that also promote literacy and cross-cultural communication. These stories serve to remind us that everyone has the potential to overcome great obstacles and achieve their dreams by following in the footsteps of heroes. MYHERO.com invites children, families, schools and organizations to take part in this interactive web project. By publicly honoring heroes on this award-winning site, you too can reward those who have made a difference.

Their hero gallery includes: angels (strangers who lift spirits and give hope through acts of kindness); animals that save lives and soothe spirits, as well as humans who devote their lives to helping animals; artists (painters, musicians, photographers, filmmakers, actors, and designers who share their talents to bring us a new vision of life); business entrepreneurs, who successfully create businesses that have regard for the social needs of the community; community leaders (citizens who contribute to their local communities in many ways); earth-keepers, who devote themselves to keeping out planet clean; explorers, who celebrate the spirit of discovery; people of faith, who get their inspiration from a higher calling; family heroes (moms, dads, grandparents, aunts, uncles, sisters, and brothers); freedom heroes (individuals who stand up for justice and humanity); heroes' (those who inspire heroes); lifesavers (lifeguards, firemen, neighbors, and strangers who go out of their way to save lives); and literary heroes (characters in books and movies who charge our imaginations). (All can be found at: www.myhero.com).

7

CITIZENSHIP

Many people in our society demonstrate little awareness of the consequences of their bad behavior—indolence, disrespect, violence—and the detrimental effect it can have on their fellow citizens. Nor do they seem to understand their responsibility to contribute to the common good of the community. Today's children need to develop that awareness and understanding and they need to begin learning at an early age. Children have an essential need to be good citizens.

*****

Most of us will never understand the "thrill" of hanging out in cemeteries. But some teens seem to find them appealing. Some even find them the perfect location for vandalism. On August 9, 2004, two boys allegedly caused between fifty thousand and seventy thousand dollars worth of damage in the Stamford Cemetery. They damaged more than 150 gravestones, some of which marked the graves of Revolutionary and Civil War soldiers. The boys, ages twelve and thirteen, were charged with second-degree criminal mischief.

Webster defines a citizen as an inhabitant of a city or town, especially one who is entitled to the rights and privileges of a freeman. However, good citizens realize that there is more to citizenship than looking out for one's self and one's rights. Good citizens recognize that they have duties and responsibilities as well. To become good citizens, children need to learn and develop responsibility, an understanding of the principle of duty, an appreciation and respect for laws, and a set of values grounded in a sense of the common good.

RESPONSIBILITY

Childhood acts as preparation for adult responsibilities. The White House Conference of 1970 recognized that children need to be involved in genuine responsibilities both at home and in school so they can learn to deal constructively with personal and social problems. When children have responsibilities, they learn how to establish priorities and organize their time.

Responsibility involves a number of things: respecting and showing compassion for others, being honest as a matter of course, showing courage in standing up for one's principles, developing self-control in acting on one's principles, and maintaining self-respect. Responsible children want to be kind, friendly, truthful, considerate, helpful to others, and respectful of the rules of fair play. Children with these qualities are not likely to resort to violence as a means of dealing with their problems. Parents want their children to be responsible, to develop the habits and strengths to act responsibly in everyday life. They teach children the difference between right and wrong, good and evil, safe and dangerous. Parents demonstrate that all behaviors, good and bad, have consequences.

DEVELOPING RESPONSIBILITY

Respect ranges from displaying everyday manners to having compassion for the suffering of another. Compassion develops from trying to see things from an other person's point of view. A small children is egocentric, and can't see another's viewpoint. However, being a great observer, your small child will get her first lessons in compassion by watching you as you react to others.

Respect entails treating others fairly, regardless of class, race, ethnicity, or gender. It includes developing tolerance for people who don't share our views, beliefs, or likes and dislikes. As children grow older, they need to realize that not all their obligations to others, such as caring for an ill family member, are chosen freely. These aspects are important because many wrongs stem from indifference to the suffering of others. Motivate children to treat others as they would want to be treated.

Teach your child good manners—please, thank you, you're welcome. Encourage her to use appropriate titles such as Mr., Mrs., and Officer, when addressing adults. Tell her to exercise good judgment when expressing feelings. If she is unhappy about someone's behavior, instruct her to criticize the actions, not the person. Act as a positive role model, and follow this advice yourself.

A child who respects himself takes satisfaction in appropriate behaviors and hard-won accomplishments. He doesn't need fancy possessions, nor do does he need to put others down to respect himself. He views selfishness, recklessness, loss of self-control, cowardice, and dishonesty as wrong and unworthy. As he grows, he develops a good conscience to guide him.

A child who respects herself respects her own health and safety. She's not willing to be manipulated by others, and she realizes that patience and tolerance do not mean allowing others to mistreat her.

Everyone fails periodically, and your child needs to have permission to fail. If she's afraid to fail, she'll be afraid to take risks, and that will inhibit her ability to succeed. Let her learn from her mistakes, and when she bounces back from them, be sure to tell her that you're proud that she's resilient. Show her how you handle problems and difficult situations. Help her to learn that problems pass; she'll recover and move on.

Help your child avoid bad thinking habits, like thinking about what he doesn't have instead of what he does have. Don't use the "starving children in India" technique. It didn't work for you growing up, so it won't work for him either. Instead, teach him to appreciate and value what he already has.

Resourcefulness means knowing when to ask for help, and knowing where to get it. Let him know that you are there for him. Prompt him to ask teachers for help when needed. Foster the use of reference books and the Internet to find answers to questions and dilemmas. Show him how you get help when you need it. Most importantly, let him know that you're not afraid to ask for it.

Everyone makes mistakes. Help your child take responsibility for her own mistakes by admitting yours. Talk about your feelings regarding the mistakes and discuss ways to make things better. When she sees you taking responsibility, she'll do likewise. Facing up to mistakes requires self-criticism and honesty. The important thing is to learn from errors and do the best to correct them, not dwell on them.

ACTING RESPONSIBLY

Responsible citizens solve problems; they don't make them. Problem solving covers a wide variety of behaviors. Older children use their problem-solving skills when a goal or the solution to a problem isn't readily apparent. Children use these skills to change the situation by changing their own behavior, the problematic situation, or the environment.

As your child grows from birth to adolescence, you need to gradually widen your his range of responsibility—feeding himself, walking, learning how to dress, doing homework, driving, and so on. The goal is that by age eighteen he can live on his own (theoretically), solve his own problems and make his own decisions. If you don't allow him to learn to solve problems and make decisions, you greatly decrease his chances of becoming a responsible adult. Your making decisions and solving problems for him has two possible outcomes: (1) he may never learn how to stand on his own two feet, and he'll have trouble living on his own because he can't make decisions; or (2) he may become rebellious, use alcohol or drugs, engage in promiscuous sex or other dangerous behaviors.

The problems your child encounter on a regular basis are like decisions; some are simple—others, complex. She runs into problems with parents, siblings, friends, school, activities, and even inanimate objects. Her approach to the problem will be influenced by the nature of the problem (simple versus complex), her experience with solving problems, and her intellectual and creative abilities.

Scientific problem solving takes place in a laboratory. It focuses on one problem, and controls as many unknowns as possible. But life isn't a laboratory. Children face problems in the real world. They most likely have a limited amount of time to solve them, and they'll be faced with unforeseeable factors and events. In a fickle world children need to be flexible. Yet, problem-solving skills don't occur in a vacuum. Children learn them by interacting with parents, other adults, siblings, and friends. The ability to solve problems typically starts during the late-school years, but you can foster these skills early on.

Studies show that young children who express their emotions freely and who have high levels of fantasy in their play tend to become creative problem-solvers. According to Sandra Russ, Ph.D., a psychologist at Case Western Reserve University, children who use high level fantasy play, such as puppets and story telling, tend to come up with different ideas by using various roles and voices—good practice for solving problems. Therefore, foster the growth of young child's problem solving skills by encouraging fantasy play. Read fairy tales and discuss them. These stimulate imagination, develop intellect, clarify emotions, reflect aspirations and anxieties, deal with frustration, and offer behavior guidelines and potential solutions to the problems that may bother her. You can also inspire imagination by having children your child develop her own stories, by using puppet play, and by using dramatic/role play (playing house, school). Whatever the fantasy play, allow her to realize that if she's confronted with the harsh realities of life, she can find ways to solve problems successfully.

As your child grows into the school-age years, help him develop actual problem-solving skills. It's typically an interpersonal process that involves seven steps:

1. Define the problem. This may sound simplistic, but many people forget this first step, only to find themselves floundering because they don't know what they're dealing with. Children can't solve a problem until they know exactly what the problem is.
2. Identify the cause of the problem. The cause is whatever brings about the problem.
3. Brainstorm and consider all possible solutions.
4. Choose a solution to try for a period of time.
5. Design a plan to carry out the solution. Identify ways to handle possible obstacles.
6. Implement the plan. This usually requires intellectual, intrapersonal, manual, or even technical skills.
7. Evaluate the outcome. If the problem is solved, move on. If not, explore alternative solutions.

Assign chores. Teach your child by assigning chores. Even a preschooler can pull a little bit of his own weight. Participating in family chores strengthens a sense of belonging and lays the foundations for the development of a sense of responsibility. Doing chores also minimizes the chance that he'll take others' efforts and contributions for granted.

When your child fulfills the responsibility of doing chores, he gains respect and learns competence. He'll soon realize that you depend on him to complete certain tasks. It's better if you start assigning chores when he is young, but it's never too late to start. Tell him that running a household is a shared family responsibility and that chores are part of family life, not punishment.

Volunteer In Your Community   Community service has become such an important experience for young people that schools across the nation have incorporated (community service) into their curriculums. Children can take part in numerous volunteer activities and then reflect on their experiences.

Volunteering teaches children and teenagers what it means to make and keep a commitment. Your child will learn how to be on time for a job, do her best, be proud of the results, and be a good citizen. She will learn that we are all collectively responsible for the well-being of our entire community. If she starts volunteering at an early age, she'll see it as a normal part of her life as she grows older.

Volunteering helps your child realize that one person can make a difference. This is an empowering message because he can see that he is important enough to have an impact on someone else. He can learn that it's good to sacrifice sometimes, to give up a toy so a less fortunate child can have one, or to give up some free time to visit a lonely elder. He can recruit other kids to help, and teach them that there are more important things in life than personal needs or desires. Community service can put your child in touch with people of different abilities, backgrounds, ethnicities, cultures, and ages. He'll notice that people have similar values and needs, and he'll develop greater tolerance.

Encourage Your Child To Get A Part-Time Job   Work teaches teens responsibility, helps them pay for their own expenses, and teaches them that money is a tool. Many teens work—half in retail stores, fast-food restaurants, and other stores, and about a quarter in service industries such as nursing homes. About 8 percent work in the agricultural industry. Work builds character, but your child's first responsibility is to get a good education. Work should never interfere with that, or with his free time. Your child will never be able to recoup his teen years.

VALUES

As traditional values vanish, they tend to be replaced by the quest for self-fulfillment, self-expression, and affluence. Self-fulfillment and self-expression can be laudable goals, but if they are our only goals, self-destruction, loneliness, and alienation can result. Hedonism encourages some people to "do their own thing," a path that can lead to chaos. Respect for individuality diminishes, and conflict ensues.

Values facilitate the integration of a child inner life with his outer behaviors. Values offer a connection from the past to the present and into the future. The values learned from parental example and teachings provide strength and affiliation. Values influence behavior, both consciously and unconsciously. If a child lacks moral integrity, he'll show little regard for people and the rights and property of others, and he'll be unable to judge behavior as right or wrong.

Values are perceptions held about the worth or importance of a certain idea, thing or person. They are the standards or principles we use to determine what is to be right and proper. Beliefs are the attitudes that reflect a person's values. When people communicate, they send messages of who they are and what they believe. Values give humans focus and serve as the guides children use in making decisions. They're learned phenomena, and shared values become fundamental to the integrity of your child, your family, and your community. People transmit values from one generation to the next, but values remain open to change because they are responsive to social contexts and situations.

A child's value creation is related to her developmental age, and her values are reflected in the behaviors she exhibits at different ages. Positive values result in healthy behaviors, especially the development of moral integrity and faith. As a child develops healthy values, she achieves a positive sense of self, internalizes the cultural values and beliefs of her social group, learns to value herself and her contribution to her family, and feels a sense of understanding and belonging to the community.

Moral integrity involves exhibiting an understanding of right and wrong, demonstrating a sense of responsibility to oneself, others, and the environment, and reflecting on the ethical issues of fairness or justice. You can enhance the development of your child's moral integrity by valuing her contributions to the family and the community, and by emotionally and intellectually rewarding her for those contributions. Children need to believe that they make a difference and have a future.

A child's moral judgment depends on his developmental stage. When young, he has little sense of right and wrong. When he gets older, especially once he reaches adolescence, he is more likely to be reflective as he examines moral dilemmas and is able to discuss and understand motivation and conditions that influence behavior.

Since values are learned from others, a newborn has none. She has not yet reached the stage of intellectual development of incorporating parental values into her behavior system. However, parent serve as models even then. By toddlerhood, a child faces limits placed on her in the form of a moral decree from parents. Parents enforce these limits to aid in her socialization in accordance with adult wishes. She develops self-control through parental efforts, but their control at this age depends on the approval or disapproval of others. Her moral behavior is also influenced by what she sees others do. If she sees parents doing something, she assumes it is acceptable. Parents can help foster her moral development at this early stage by modeling and praising her for what she does right, and by disciplining her for what she does do wrong. These help to teach her right from wrong.

A preschooler begins to demonstrate some internal control over his behavior, but these controls aren't always consistent or effective. He may even be very strict, developing an overwhelming feeling of guilt when his behavior doesn't match his internal control system. Moral behavior continues to be influenced by parental modeling, as well as modeling from others including baby-sitters and the television—warranting you to be careful with your selection of sitters and TV shows. During the preschool years, he controls his behavior because he desires parental love and approval. His moral choices involve simple activities, such as sharing and taking turns. He learns that people have rights and desires that are as important as his own rights and desires. He expresses his values by stating who or what he likes or what he wants to be when he grows up (but these values can change rapidly, even within minutes).

A school-age child makes moral decisions every day—whether or not to cheat on a test, whether to tell the teacher that she saw a friend cheating on a test, whether or not to share, whether or not to have a cookie before dinner after being told not to. She sees behavior as being either right or wrong, but as she reaches the middle years, she begins to weigh several aspects of a situation. At first she believes that an act is wrong because it brings on displeasure or punishment from an adult; later she develops the insight to see that an act is wrong because it breaks a rule, harms another person, or violates another person's rights. By the time she's ten or eleven, she'll be able to place herself in someone else's position, and she will begin to exercise the rule of "doing unto others as you would have them do unto you."

During the adolescent years, a teen acquires a set of ideals—a system of values derived from what he believes could be, not necessarily from what is. He may associate his beliefs with a particular religion, philosophical school of thought, social movement, or other form of organization that provides a basis for ideals. He will use these beliefs in weighing decisions about what's right and wrong, important and not important, or best and worst. His ideal system may change several times over the course of adolescence, providing him with a range of experiences on which to base later choices.

TEACHING VALUES

As a parent, you probably believe that teaching your children values is one of your most meaningful undertakings and a good way to make a lasting contribution to society. You want your child to have firm values, and you realize that it's not an easy task.

Respect your child and require respect in return. Be fair. Relate to her on her own level, and make allowances for the immaturity of her developmental stage. Insist on courtesy and expect consideration. Require that special respect that is due you as a parent, as well as the simple respect you are due as a human being.

Base your disciplinary measures on respect, restraint, gentleness, and fairness. As your child gets older, ask for and consider her opinions. Remember that morality develops in stages that have their foundation in secure attachment and trust. At each stage your child has her own ideas of right and wrong and different reasons why a person should be good, and each stage brings her closer to mature moral development.

The surest way to help your child develop values and moral reasoning is to teach by example. Be aware that he is watching how you treat others, and how you lead your life. Think back to how your own parents influenced your moral development and values by their behavior and the examples they set. Clear picture, isn't it? Your behavior will be etched just as clearly in your child's mind.

But teaching by example is not enough because your child will be surrounded by bad examples as well as good. He needs your words as well as your actions. He needs to know why living by his values is important. He needs to know what lies beneath those values. Use children's books, stories, movies, and open conversation to discuss morality. Worship and celebrate your faith together as a family—a great way to develop morality.

If your children are not growing up to be good, honest, kind, self-disciplined, hard-working citizens, their humanity becomes diminished.

Promote moral development by fostering the following characteristics: compassion, justice, generosity, honesty and trustworthiness, courage, loyalty, and pride.

- Compassion: Empathy, your child's ability to put herself in anther persons shoes, is one of the most important virtues she can have. Encourage her to treat others with kindness. When she misbehaves toward another person, ask her to think about how that other person feels. You want her to realize (and care about) the consequences of her actions. Inspire her to do kind deeds, even when she's young. She can invite a newcomer over to play or create a greeting card for a shut-in. Very young children feel concern for people who suffer, build on this for your child. Discuss famous altruists such as Mother Theresa, and talk to her about people she admires. Give her books about compassionate behavior (but make sure that the characters are realistic, ordinary heroes and not the goody-two-shoes type). Limit her TV viewing to nonviolent programs where characters commit acts of kindness, instead of violence. Children tend to mimic acts of kindness when they see them.
- Justice: Compassion leads to fairness and a sense of justice. Your child should value equal treatment of himself and others without favoritism or prejudice. He must learn to be open to the comments, beliefs, and practices of others, and he should make decisions on facts, including opposing viewpoints. Blame should not given inappropriately, and (whenever possible) punishment should be natural and logical outcomes of the misbehaviors.
- Generosity: Your young child cannot give of herself or her possessions; therefore, you need to teach her about generosity. Get her into a preschool or a play group when she is three. Your child will realize that she won't be very popular if she doesn't share. By the time she's five, teach her the meaning of generosity by praising her when they demonstrate it, and by pointing out its effects. As she grows, encourage her to give to others. She can save some of her allowance, collect bottles, or perform little jobs for money that she can either give outright to the poor or disadvantaged or use to purchase food or other supplies for the needy. Advocate volunteering her time for service, as previously noted.
- Honesty: The truth comes naturally to a young child. Praise him for being honest, and honesty will become part of his character.

Remember, during his preschool years, he will be filled with fantasy, allowing him to explore the limits of reality. Therefore, he will stretch the truth and lie to create his fantasy world. Encourage his fantasies, then kindly point out reality when necessary. Don't punish or humiliate him when he lies out of fantasy. If you do, you risk the chance of his becoming a chronic liar when he grows up. During the school years, he will tend to be pretty reliable, as truth and rules are important during that stage. But once adolescence rolls around, the truth may take a back seat as he tests which limits he can stretch. However, if you instilled a good sense of honesty when he was young, his honesty will resurface. Honesty encompasses trustworthiness. He should follow through with what he says he will do—and so should you to set an example. Keeping promises and being dependable are important, as are being honest with himself and others.

- Courage: The ability to face a crisis with optimism, or the mental, physical and moral strength in the face of danger—courage becomes a critical value in today's turbulent world. Courage does not mean physically fighting back and risking serious consequences. Your child needs to know that courage sometimes means turning the other cheek and walking away. Teach her that the most important type of courage is the courage of her convictions, standing up for what she believes in. This can be difficult when she needs to stand up for her beliefs against those of her friends. Peer pressure is powerful, but not impossible to deal with. Praise her for holding up her end by telling her you know that it's difficult for her to be the only one in her group to have to follow certain rules. Display courage yourself in the face of adversity, such as job loss or financial difficulties.
- Loyalty and pride: Strengthen your family bonds by recognizing the importance of family pride and loyalty. These two values champion family stability and enable you to celebrate each family member's successes. Pride in his heritage encourages your child to seek out his roots and explore his attachment to the generations before him. This sense of pride also includes humility, the feeling that comes to him when he realizes that he is part of something greater than himself. Spend time together to build family strength. Laugh together and cry together to give him a sense of belonging. Attend events and activities that involve another family member and cheer her on. Celebrate family occasions, such as birthdays,

anniversaries, and promotions. Create and display a family tree, and discuss it. Have him obtain an oral history of your family by interviewing and recording older relatives. He could ask about their memories of marriage, children, chores, school, work, and other activities and relationships. He could then write it all down in a journal or diary. A valued past lays the foundation for a valued future.

FURTHERING CITIZENSHIP

Children learn about their country in school. They learn about those who fought to keep their country free, so that they can enjoy the rights and privileges of citizenship. But these concepts need to be reinforced at home. Holidays, such as the Fourth of July and Veterans Day in the US, and Canada Day in Canada, need to be more than just days off from school. Parents should reinforce the meaning of national citizenship.

Leah Davis, MEd, offered twenty activities for schools to use to foster citizenship in children. These are adapted here for you to use with your children:

1. Discuss what citizenship means, and include rights and responsibilities of citizens.
2. Define a good citizen and have your child share his personal stories about when he exhibited citizenship, such as following safety rules, giving toys to needy children, or helping to clean up a park.
3. Ask your child to describe what would happen if there were no rules at home, in school, or in the community.
4. Involve her in making family rules and discuss why these rules are important. Have her make up consequences that can be used if the rules are broken.
5. Ask him to interview a veteran, immigrant, or person who lived through a difficult period in history, such as the Great Depression or the Holocaust. Work together to make a list of questions he could ask such as:
   Tell me about your life?
   What was a difficult time for you?
   What does being a citizen mean to you?
6. Have her write a poem, story, play or song about citizenship. Encourage her to perform her creation for others.

7. Ask him to search for a local citizen who generously contributes to the good of the community, and send that person a thank you letter.
8. Together, read and discuss newspaper articles on various topics concerning civic life.
9. Ask her to create a home movie on your country (or on citizenship).
10. Work together with his teachers to invite speakers to share their knowledge of American or Canadian history or to portray historical characters.
11. Read stories about extraordinary Americans or Canadians and then act out the stories.
12. Discuss one of the country's founding documents.
13. Work together with members of the community to take photographs in the community for a book entitled "Our Freedoms," "Our Citizens," or another related topic.
14. Take her to attend a city council meeting, school board meeting or court session. Visit a nearby historical museum, monument, and/or national park.
15. Sing patriotic songs on national holidays.
16. Research the meaning of national symbols.
17. Create a presentation to teach others about the American or Canadian Flag, its history, symbolism, and proper care and display.
18. Talk about how taxes are used by local, state, and national governments.
19. Encourage your child to run for school office.
20. Encourage her to participate in community service projects such as recycling, picking up litter, and volunteering for other worthwhile projects.

Part Three
Enrichment Needs (Individual)

8

SPIRITUALITY

Spiritual wellness is marked by the capacity for compassion, love, altruism, forgiveness, joy and fulfillment, and is an antidote to fear, anxiety, self-absorption, anger, cynicism, and pessimism. Spirituality can transcend individuals to become a common bond between people. Some people look to organized religions to develop spiritual health, while others find meaning and purpose in their lives on their own through meditation, nature, art, or good works. Robert Coles, author of *The Spiritual Life of Children*, notes that, regardless of their cultural or religious background, children feel a profound desire to understand the universe and their place in it. That desire, expressed through words, gestures, drawings and songs, is universal. Children have an essential need for spirituality.

*****

Chris said he had to tell me something. He motioned for me to come closer, and then whispered how he hoped things would be for his parents and sister after he died. A few days later, after Chris had fought his valiant battle, leukemia claimed his young life. Working with Chris was a difficult experience, but it was also a privilege. He was sad and fearful about leaving his family behind, but he had a peaceful acceptance that was quite spiritual and is often lacking in adults. That innate sense of spirituality experienced by Chris should be nurtured in every child so that it flourishes throughout childhood and the rest of life.

Professionals have given little attention to the concept of spiritual distress in children. Some have noted various levels of spiritual distress in chronically or terminally ill children, children from disruptive families, children experiencing extreme crises such as the terrorist attack on 9/11, and children abused by the clergy. In a study of 26 boys and men sexually abused by Catholic priests, more than half of the men spoke directly about a loss of spiritual life. For most, it resulted in a disconnection from the Church—a refusal to attend mass or participate in any church activities. Others spoke of losing their belief in God, saying, "If the right hand of God can do what he did to me, then there is no God," or "What kind of God would allow this to happen to children in His name?" Others decided to transfer their loyalties to other organized religions but spoke about their mistrust of Catholic priests. Many of them lost their trust, not only in priests, but in all authority figures.

THE NATURE OF SPIRITUALITY

Spirituality goes beyond religious affiliation. Spirituality, even for those people who do not believe in God, involves a striving for inspiration, reverence, meaning, purpose and a sense of awe. Spirituality involves trying to be in harmony with the universe, and searching for answers about the infinite. These efforts can become particularly focued when a person faces stress, illness, or death. Deeply spiritual people feel that they are not alone in times of crisis, while those having an underdeveloped spirituality may feel alone and hopeless, without purpose or meaning in their lives. Victor Frankel, author of *Man's Search for Meaning*, states that when life has no meaning, it becomes empty. He calls this an "existential vacuum,"—a state of inertia, boredom, and apathy. If this state persists, it progresses into existential frustration, and people try (unsuccessfully) to fill the emptiness with drugs, violence, food, over-work, and/or other activities.

The positive characteristics of a healthy spirituality include a sense of wholeness and harmony with one's self, with others, and with a higher power. Depending on their developmental level, people experience and project strong identity, personal security, and a sense of hope. This does not mean that these individuals feel totally satisfied with life or that they know all the answers. Everyone has times of anxiety, help-lessness, and confusion. These difficult situations generate spiritual questions and help people realize that their spirituality is valid, charac-terized by:

- HOLISM. Holism involves perceiving the universe as a system of harmonious interconnectedness (rather than simply the sum of its parts),—integrating body, mind, and spirit.
- FAITH. Faith is belief in the strength and presence of a higher power (which might or might not be a person). Faith enables a person to believe that a higher power helps her in times of trouble, sorrow, and pain, and that this higher power will never forget or abandon her. (Some researchers believe that faith can increase the body's resistance to stress.)
- HOPE. Hope is often experienced as trust in God's mercy, wis-dom, and justice. Hope allows and encourages handing problems over to the care of this benevolent higher power. Without hope—that positive attitude held in the face of difficulty—a per-son can become depressed and prone to illness.
- LOVE. Love is manifested as care for, concern about, and generos-ity toward others. Love is altruistic and giving, and makes a differ-ence in others' lives. (A close network of supportive family and friends sharing their loving attention, can offer protection against many diseases. Research shows that people who experience love and support tend to resist unhealthy behaviors and feel less stressed.)
- FORGIVENESS. Forgiveness is a creative release of hostility and resentment over some past hurt. This doesn't mean that the forgiv-ing person must forget the event. It simply means that he lets go of any revenge fantasies, resentment, or bitterness against the per-son that caused the harm. (A Stanford University study found that college students trained to forgive were significantly less angry, more hopeful, and better able to deal with emotions than students not trained to forgive.) Forgiving frees up a great deal of energy that can be used in more positive ways.
- SPIRITUAL WELL-BEING. Spiritual well-being is experienced as peace, harmony, an affirmation of life, and a sense of interconnect-edness with God, self, community, and nature. In a study of older adults, researchers found that harmony and interconnectedness were the two major determinants of spiritual well-being in those who were terminally ill, as well as in those who were healthy.

HOW SPIRITUALITY DEVELOPS
OVER THE LIFESPAN

Theologian James Fowler shed light on the development of spirituality by identifying stages in the development of faith. Fowler conceives of faith as a self-constructed "self-discernment system" the aim of which is to extract guidance and meaning from the significant relationships or "centers of power" in ones life. Growing in faith is a universally experienced process that is not necessarily religious. It's an important part of everyday life that serves to organize the wholeness of our lives and that gives rise to our most comprehensive frames of meaning. Faith involves our ego, conscious and unconscious thought, emotions, reasoning, perceptions, and sense of identity.

According to Fowler, each stage of development, an individual develops a reliance on or an attachment to what he considers to be the new center of power, whether person, symbol, or philosophy. Religion or creed may become the center of power at any stage, but a person relates to religious doctrine differently at each level. Fowler suggests that most middle-class American churches and synagogues foster functioning at stage three or a little beyond, and that one would have trouble achieving stages five and six without a concept of an Ultimate Being or God.

According to Fowler, an individual begins life in a primal or undifferentiated stage with a lack of clarity among the five domains (biophysical, cognitive, social, affective, and spiritual) and between the self, the significant other, and the supraordinate values that govern the relationship between them. As each stage emerges, these three basic elements become more clearly differentiated and then gradually reintegrated, with the last stage representing a highly integrated union of the five domains, the self, significant other, and motivating values. Regardless of religious or cultural beliefs, people who master the last stage closely resemble each other in both structure and content of faith.

STAGE ZERO: PRIMAL OR UNDIFFERENTIATED FAITH (BIRTH TO TWO YEARS):

The main psychological task of this period is the development of trust in the world as a good place where the infant's needs are met. The strength of trust, autonomy, hope, and courage developed in this stage underlie all of later faith development. An infant's experiences in this stage have a tremendous influence on his ability to trust his caregivers and may later affect his ability to trust God. For example, if an infant is abused by parents, that infant's ability to trust may be seriously compromised. Because many religions depict God or a Higher Power as a loving parent worthy of our trust, anything that damages a child's ability to trust his caregivers may have equally devastating consequences on his ability to let go and completely trust God to meet his needs.

STAGE ONE: INTUITIVE-PROJECTIVE FAITH (TWO TO SIX YEARS):

During this stage, a young child makes conscious attempts to give meaning to experiences and relationships. She combines fragments of cultural images and stories into her own significant associations dealing with God and what is sacred. (Because they receive so much information about God through language, television, holidays, and so on, few Western children—even when they have no formal religious instruction—reach school age without some concept of God.) A preschooler's magical thinking creates powerful fantasy-filled concepts of supernatural events from cultural narratives. She begins to develop awareness of self, death, sex, and the strong cultural and familial taboos developed around these issues. New images of God are formed through ritual play, storytelling, and fantasy, and these images are often symbolic and archetypal in nature. (If too much emphasis is placed on negative archetypal images such as the "devil" and the "suffering of hell," a narrow and rigid faith may develop.)

STAGE TWO: MYTHICAL-LITERAL FAITH (SIX TO TWELVE YEARS):

At this stage, a school-age child begins to take on the beliefs, stories, and observations that belong to their community. His major task is to develop the ability to separate reality from make-believe. Reciprocal fairness, and justice based on reciprocity, are overriding concepts. At this stage, he tends to be quite literal and to anthropomorphize the characters in his narratives as a way of finding meaning and coherence in his experiences. (Children abused at this stage often decide that they must have deserved it because God is fair and would not allow something unfair to happen. They thus may get stuck at this stage and develop into over-controlling, perfectionistic, and work-oriented adults.)

STAGE THREE: SYNTHETIC-CONVENTIONAL FAITH (AGE TWELVE AND BEYOND—UNTIL A PERSON ENTERS STAGE 4):

A teenager gradually begins to find a need for a more personal relationship with the unifying power, and thus, she begins to appraise herself along the guidelines and through the eyes of others. She takes active measures to change herself to meet the approval of the significant other. She believes that the other (whether a person, the culture, or God) knows what's best. This stage is characterized by a religious hunger for a God who knows, accepts, and validates the self. A teen sees God as a divinely personal significant other in her life. She is aware she has values, can articulate and defend those values, and usually feels quite passionate about them. However, she has not yet questioned or evaluated the system to which she adheres because to do so would place her outside her religious group. Thus she would risk losing the community, which, at this stage of life, defines her. The main danger at this stage of faith development is that the individuation process may be arrested. Betrayals can lead to despair and distrust, and may prevent the development of the teen's personal relationship with God. Without this sense of a personal relationship with God, the individual cannot progress to the next stage.

STAGE FOUR: INDIVIDUATIVE-REFLECTIVE FAITH: (EARLY ADULTHOOD AND BEYOND—UNTIL A PERSON ENTERS STAGE FIVE OR TO THE END OF LIFE):

At this stage, a young adult begins to examine his value system, break his reliance on an external source of authority, differentiate between symbol and meaning, and assume a new authority and responsibility for himself. Identity becomes regrounded as he revels in this ability to assume responsibility for value orientation and choices. Roles and relationships become expressions of identity rather than crutches for it. A young adult is vulnerable to the self-deception that forgets the "mystery of his own consciousness." In the process, he may lose his sense of community as he relinquishes symbols and rituals in search of meaning created through his own power and control. Many adults will spend the rest of their lives at this stage, a stage characterized by dichotomous thinking ("either this is true or that is true" rather than "it is possible that both of these apparently contradictory concepts are true at the same time"—the latter position characterizes stage 5). Stage four is also characterized by questioning and testing the values one has been taught (e.g., symbols and rituals are often seen as empty and meaningless). Ideally, a young adult takes the opinions of others into consideration as he makes decisions and takes responsibility for his choices. Nevertheless, there must be a critical distancing from the previous value system in order for him to develop his own relationship with God. It's easy to wrap up a little package that becomes flat and sterile, a world of black and white, with explanations that become an end in themselves, empty of meaning. Disillusionment with earlier religious dogma, philosophies, or relationships can lead to expressions of anger, hostility and self-aggrandizement. On the other hand, a young adult can create a coherent, life-enhancing set of beliefs by analyzing and reworking the faith inherited from others. He may end up with the same set of beliefs he had as a child, but it's now his personal system and not merely an extension of his parents' system. (There is also a danger for an individual who remains stuck at this stage. He may develop a tendency to overintellectualize faith at the expense of feelings and emotions.)

STAGE FIVE: CONJUNCTIVE FAITH (MIDLIFE AND BEYOND—UNTIL A PERSON ENTERS STAGE SIX OR UNTIL THE END OF LIFE):

Faith moves beyond the black and white logic of stage four because of the increased ability and willingness to see many sides of an issue simultaneously. In midlife, an adult tries to see the total structure before categorizing. She lets the truth of a message or Scripture speak for itself. She appreciates symbols, myths, and rituals, both hers and others', because she grasps the depth of the reality to which these symbols point. Awe of the Holy and a reverence for paradox emerge (as the ultimate truth is seen to transcend temporal constraints). She moves beyond the norms of a reference group to the truth of other traditions. This does not mean that she loses commitment to her own traditions. Instead, it means she is more open to expanding the truth. (Because of the complexity of this faith level, few people reach it before midlife.)

STAGE SIX: UNIVERSALIZING FAITH (MIDLIFE AND BEYOND):

This final, mature form of faith is rare. Only a handful of people achieve it, and most of them become martyrs. They assume a spiritual stance of pure conscientiousness, and their involvement in the life and concerns of others is unmindful of their own needs or self-preservation. Occasionally, events place them in the forefront of political unrest or social injustice. Because this stage is also marked by a disregard for society's institutions, they can be seen as threatening to society as a whole. These can be people who, like Mahatma Ghandi and Martin Luther King, become martyrs for a cause. Others, like Mother Theresa, live by a greater vision than themselves, living the kingdom of God as a means of overcoming division, oppression, and brutality.

Fowler believes that each successive stage represents growth toward a more mature response to God, and toward more consistently humane caring for other human beings.

NURTURING SPIRITUALITY

By nurturing spirituality in a child, parents contribute to that child's sense of personal value, her sense of belonging in the world, and her belief that she has a capacity for joy and fulfillment.

To nurture you child's spirituality, follow these guidelines:
- Continue to develop *your* spirituality. We all have the capacity for good and bad, but the way you choose to live is what your child learns from. This begins at an early age to influence her values, attitudes, and reactions to various situations.
- Recognize and share the spiritual reality in everyday life—the blueness of the sky, a cold glass of water, the change of the seasons.
- Since most religions do not begin instruction until children are at least of preschool age, start your own teaching earlier. As noted by Fowler, this begins with the closeness of your interactions as soon as your child is born. Continue by showing (and telling about) the virtues of generosity, thankfulness, trust, sacrifice, honor, faith, hope, and love.
- Listen. Allow your child to share his thoughts, feelings, and whims in a relaxed environment.
- Provide quiet reflection time, especially at night, and encourage her to reflect upon her day.
- Share words of love and acceptance.
- Read spiritual books together, such as *Cassandra's Angel* and *The Big, Big Sea* for a young child, and *The Journey Home* for an older child.

- Pray together. Shared prayer is one of the deepest and most intimate forms of communication.
- Show respect for all family members and others.
- As your child grows, help him negotiate between the dominant American culture and the countervailing values of the communities of faith.
- Foster a sense of community by volunteering with your child. Even a small child can participate by donating old toys and clothes to children in need.
- Engage in your faith together. Actively participate in religious functions, holidays and rituals, and explain their meaning to your child.
- Make each day a new beginning. It's not the end of the world if you lose your temper or make a mistake. Start over. Forgiveness and faith means knowing that spirituality moves and breathes and is our life force.

Spirituality is the foundation upon which we build self-esteem, values, morals, and a sense of belonging. It gives life direction and meaning. Thus it is essential that parents nurture their children's spirituality.

9

CREATIVITY

Thomas Edison, Winston Churchill, Enrico Caruso, and Walt Disney are just four examples of famous people whose creative genius went unnoticed during childhood. All children have an essential need to have opportunities for creative thought and expression, whether or not they are geniuses-in-training.

*****

Once upon a time, there lived fierce dragons, spirited princesses, and towering flowers that sang a cappella. They all frolicked in the Imagine Nation, a country that proudly flourished in the minds of children. Its tiny leaders demonstrated the utmost cleverness in their intellectual, emotional, and social prowess. They could transform themselves from fearful tikes to mighty defenders; from failures to champions—no problem was insurmountable. They viewed the universe through rainbow lenses, blurring reality and fantasy into endless possibilities. There was no stopping them.

Until the grown-ups came along
The grown-ups, with all their good intentions, sought to take over the Imagine Nation. After all, grown-ups knew what was best—clear boundaries between reality and fantasy, structure, grown-up leaders,

and lots, and lots of tools and how-to rules. They praised the virtues of innovation, yet preferred the comfort of routine and conformity. They constantly stood guard to assure that the children took no risks. They evaluated the children's every move, rewarding mediocrity to the fullest, so that the children focused more on how they were doing instead of the pure joy of accomplishment and the pleasures of creative activities. Originality became a mistake, and exploration a waste of time.

And so, the Imagine Nation crumbled. The dragons died, the princesses gave up their thrones, and the flowers refused to sing. The children became shells of their former selves and mere clones of the grown-ups—restrictive, competitive, pressurized, passionless, and so very boring.

THE MAGIC OF A CHILD'S IMAGINATION

Parents often speak of their children's active imaginations, noting that their kids are creative, naturally curious, and playful. To be imaginative means that children formulate varied and rich mental images, see beyond the obvious, and draw upon their experiences in inventive and effective ways. Studies of children's brain activity actually offer evidence that children do indeed have active imaginations. Children experience theta wave activity (the brain stage that brings forward heightened receptivity, flashes of dreamlike imagery, inspiration, and long-forgotten memories) even when awake. (Adults primarily experience this stage when their minds hover between being awake and falling asleep.) Therefore, it would seem that children are more adept than adults at forming varied and unusual images.

While it's true that adults have the advantage when it comes to storing and retrieving information, drawing from experience and making appropriate and effective judgments, children are not bothered by inconsistencies, departures from conventions, and nonliteralness. Young children can't always distinguish fantasy from reality, allowing ideas to slip from one realm into the other, responding in ways that some adults find enviable.

IMAGINATION IS LIKE A MUSCLE—IF YOU DON'T USE IT, YOU LOSE IT

An active imagination is the heart of creativity. Yet, according to experts at the National Association of School Psychologists, the personality traits that some creative children develop are often viewed as strange or unproductive:

- Free thinking: Creative children appear undisciplined and lacking in goal orientation.
- Gullibility: Creative children become excited over "half-baked" ideas and may not see the flaws or drawbacks that adults would easily see.
- Humor: Creative children discover humor in ideas that adults consider very serious. The children's ability to question and see other perspectives may be interpreted as mocking or obnoxious.
- Daydreaming: Creative children learn and solve problems through fantasy. Mind wandering bolsters creativity, but it also makes children appear spacey and inattentive.
- Aloneness: Creative children need to be alone to allow their ideas to emerge, but society's emphasis on togetherness stifles this.
- Activity: Creative children typically develop ideas while "doing nothing." Then, once the idea materializes, they become absorbed in the activity. This fluctuation from one extreme to another is confusing and frustrating to others.

And yet these personality traits are tolerated, even respected, in adults we consider to be "creative geniuses!"

CREATIVE DEFINITIONS

Defining creativity can prove to be stifling. Creativity has been described in terms of process, product, or person, and as the interpersonal and intrapersonal process by which original, high quality, and significant products are developed. But this focuses exclusively on inventors whose products have revolutionized society. Even when people revel in the creative contributions of adults, they often view creative thought in children as frivolous, aimless and counteractive to the attainment of academic standards.

Some consider creativity a gift from God. The form of this gift—musical, spatial, motoric, linguistic—varies from person to person. And it is the challenge of parents, teachers, and others to recognize, foster, and nourish each child's creative capacity. In this respect, nourishing creativity is nothing less than an appreciation of the miracles of God's creation.

Creativity differs from intelligence and talent. Highly creative children may not be highly intelligent or talented, and highly intelligent children may not be creative. Talent refers to the possession of a high degree of technical skill in one area, such as music or art. To confuse matters, creativity can be evidenced not only in art, music and writing, but also in science, social studies, and other areas, including everyday activities. Think of how creative you must be to stretch the household budget, vary the ways you cook chicken, or keep your old clunker road-worthy.

Creativity should be viewed as a process in children, a process that generates ideas. Creativity is a child's original way of looking at things, the way she adds something new to what already exists. A child's response may be either popular or original, the latter being creative. For example, I asked my nephew Christopher, age ten, and my nieces Gianna and Daniella, ages eight and four, respectively, "What kinds of things are round?" They began with popular answers such as the earth, balls, plates, and coins. But once their creative juices began to flow, they spontaneously shouted original answers that included fish, zeros, pies, bongo drums, tires, pupils (as in eyes), binoculars, pizza, and the highly creative answers—pepperoni slices, toilet seats, and nostrils.

The Association for Childhood Education International (ACEI) proposes that the definition of creativity be enriched and enlarged to be consistent with contemporary research and that it not be dependent on talent alone, but also on motivation, interest, effort, and opportunity. They note that the creative process is socially supported, culturally influenced, and collaboratively achieved, and propose that creativity be reconceptualized along at least five dimensions:

1. Use the word "creative" in combination with "thought". This helps to clear up misconceptions that creativity is elusive and nondescriptive, and that creative people are ineffective free spirits. Creative thought is synonymous with productive thought because it's based on complex reasoning processes.
2. Recognize that creative potential alone cannot bring ideas to fruition. Creative thinking can be underdeveloped, diminished, and even ruined. Thus, it must be nurtured and developed.
3. Differentiate the "Big C Creativity" of celebrated geniuses from the "Little c Creativity" that is widely distributed among people. We should value the "Little c." Its contributions may not be spectacular, but they are significant.

4. Gain a multicultural and global perspective on creativity. Western thought emphasizes invention, individual achievement, and linear thinking (thinking in one direction), while other cultures value more open thought processes and creativity as a group process.
5. Acknowledge that capturing the essence of creative endeavors mandates a blurring of traditional disciplinary boundaries. Creativity is not restricted to the fine arts.

BENEFITS OF CREATIVITY

Creativity is the freest form of self-expression for children, and there is nothing more fulfilling for children than to be able to express themselves freely. Creative people:

- are more psychologically healthy;
- have a continued appreciation for what goes on around them;
- see more and are more open to new experiences;
- are better at expressing and coping with their feelings;
- don't fear the unknown and are risk takers;
- often use humor to express ideas;
- don't need to minimize uncertainty or avoid it (they actually find it attractive);
- are better problem solvers, producing solutions that go beyond the usual constraints of time, place, common materials, and uses of objects;
- enjoy the messiness and exploration involved in creativity;
- are more energetic and flexible;
- have more faith and confidence in their impulses;
- develop a greater sense of self-discovery;
- seem to have more self-confidence and greater assertiveness.

Creativity helps children grow, view things in new and unusual ways, see problems that no one else knows exists, and find effective ways to solve these problems.

HOW WE STIFLE CREATIVITY IN CHILDREN

Despite the fact that we claim to value creativity, we blatantly develop ways to crush it at home and at school. Young children love to learn in creative ways—manipulating objects, experimenting, telling stories, dancing, making believe. But adults like conforming behaviors—courtesy, obedience, following rules, punctuality. While these behaviors are important, they become all-consuming, pushing creative thought into the far corners of children's minds, so much so that by age nine or ten, children experience what's called the "fourth-grade slump," marked by a significant reduction in creative productivity. Pressures to conform increase through adolescence, and some children never get out of their slump, causing them to grow into conventional and "ordinary" adults.

I require a creative project in my pediatric nursing course; a course where the majority of students are young adults, ages nineteen to twenty one. The assignment reads:

> "Each student is required to complete a creative project for a specific age group between the ages of two and sixteen years. The project should be designed to teach the child something about a safety, a psychiatric problem or a developmental issue, reflecting the student's knowledge of both the issue and child development. For example, you can teach twelve-year-olds about bicycle safety, five-year-olds about germs and handwashing, or nine-year-olds about puberty. You can be as imaginative as possible, but the project must include the following:
>
> 1. A double-spaced, two-page write-up that explains how the project is appropriate for the age group and issue chosen.
> 2. A Reference list with at least five references, APA style, attached to the two-page write-up.
> 3. A ten minute presentation that covers the following:
>   a. why you chose this age group,
>   b. why you chose this topic,
>   c. why the project is appropriate for the age group,
>   d. the actual project.
>
> Project ideas include: making a doll or toy; creating a game; writing a children's book; writing a short story for older children or teens; creating a few songs, drawings, a new sport, a photo series, a short video, or whatever else you can come up with!"

Some students come up with wonderfully creative projects, such as the "Puberty Board Game" for teaching kids about their changing bodies, "Chemo-tag", a game, that physically demonstrates how chemotherapy works, and a terrific array of picture and story books. Not too surprisingly, few students are concerned about the left-brain concepts related to child development and the content of their teaching topic; most are concerned with the creative aspect, usually pleading for ideas! Drawing, storytelling, and creating toys or games have become frightening (instead of fun) by the time many students reach college.

Just how do we stifle creativity in children? Anecdotal notes and research, by Marvin Bartel, Schlomit Avshalom, and Hennessy and Amabile tell us that creativity "killers" are commonplace at home and in schools:

- Lack of balance: Overemphasis on linear thinking, rules and conformity, diminish creative flow.
- Surveillance: Hovering over children makes them feel they are constantly being observed while working. Constant surveillance diminishes risk taking and dampens creative urges.
- Evaluation: When kids feel they must continuously worry about how they're doing, they ignore the satisfaction that comes with their accomplishments.
- Rewards: Excessive accolades and prizes distract children from the intrinsic pleasure of creative activity.
- Competition: A win-lose situation where only one person comes out on top denies the process of children progressing at their own rates.
- Over-control: Constantly telling kids what to do makes them feel that their originality is a mistake and that exploration is a waste of time. Instructing children as to what activities to choose instead of allowing them to follow their own curiosities and passions restricts the active exploration and experimentation that might lead to creative discovery and production.
- Pressure: Grandiose expectations of a child's performance, which often go beyond a child's developmental capabilities, can instill an aversion for the activity. Children feel pressured to perform and conform within strictly prescribed guidelines that again deter experimentation, exploration, and innovation.
- Systematization: The overuse of workbooks and formal skill development can stifle the imagination. They force children to develop convergent thinking skills, which produce one correct answer to a question and are characteristic of the thinking required for standardized intelligence testing. However, children

also need to develop divergent thinking skills, which produce many answers to the same question and are more characteristic of creativity.

- Television and computers: The use of TV and computers forces children to sit passively, with little or no involvement needed to make the action occur. (Even interactive video games, are programmed with a level of forced choices, requiring little creativity.)
- Praising neatness and conformity over expressiveness: Neatness truly is overrated!
- Answering all the questions: Children cannot learn creative problem-solving if we prevent them from exploring alternative answers and options.

CULTIVATING CREATIVITY

Creativity is a form of self-expression that requires time, space, and the freedom to commit oneself to the effort it takes to make the creative activity one's own. Creative activities acknowledge and celebrate the uniqueness and diversity of each child, and provide excellent opportunities to individualize your parenting to focus on each of your children.

Time is one of the most important ingredients of creativity. Give your child plenty of it. Children enter the ultimate state of creativity known as "flow" more naturally than adults. Kids easily get lost in what they're doing. In flow, there is no time, just the moment at hand. Adults are less comfortable with flow because they are more conscious of time. This discomfort often causes adults to interrupt children during creative moments, tearing them out of their deep concentration. Kids can become frustrated when interrupted in the middle of something they love, stifling the creative flow.

Other ways to nurture creativity include the following:

- Maintain balance. Creativity should have equal footing with intellect and rule-following.
- Be supportive of your child's creativity. Let him explore a range of activities to find his strength and passion. The essentials of childhood creativity—finding his passions, mastering the skills needed to follow that passion, and collaborating with others—are all prerequisites for creativity in adult life.

- Tolerate the unusual. Let your child know that it's not always crucial to have the right answer. Value novel, innovative, and unique approaches as well.
- Let her be messy! Disorder and chaos are part of the creative process.
- Resist the temptation to overcrowd your child's schedule with organized activities.
- Set up a creative atmosphere. Provide plenty of safe supplies—paints, clay, dress-up clothes, photographs, wood, paper, music—and experiences such as backyard explorations, and trips to zoos and museums. Keep the experiences varied. Multi-ethnic, multicultural, and other community and everyday life experiences provide a greater range of creative expression.
- Encourage active pursuits and creative movement. Passive activities rely on other people's ideas and images and require no physical activity. Use games such as role-play, follow the leader, and guess what I am, to develop large muscles along with creativity. Building with sand, clay and mud also stimulates muscle activity.
- Be a good adult role model. Stay open to new ideas and experiences, and share your creative interests with your children.

CREATIVE STUFF

YOUNG KIDS	OLDER KIDS
Visually interesting objects	Fashion design
Clay	Playing musical instrument
Finger paints	Art
Crayons	Animation
Markers	Creating comic strips
Blocks	Dance
Dress-up	Songwriting
Treasure hunts	Writing movie scripts/making their
Creating simple recipes	own movies or TV shows
Storytelling	Cooking
Making up songs	Sewing
Backyard (public park) adventures	Quilting
Playing zoo or jungle creatures	Knitting/crocheting

Encourage kids of all ages to come up with their own ideas, inventions, artistic expressions and science projects.

Don't force your child to engage in creative activities if she is not interested. Creativity is a pleasure to be enjoyed, not a chore to endure.

ODYSSEY OF THE MIND

Looking for a way for your child to really test her creative skills? Odyssey of the Mind is an international program that provides creative problem-solving opportunities for students from kindergarten through college. Kids use their creativity to solve problems that range from building a mechanical device to presenting their own interpretation of a literary classic. Thousands of teams from throughout the US, and from about twenty-five other countries, participate in the program, bringing their solutions to competition on local, state, national, and international levels.

Odyssey of the Mind is competitive, but their competitive element encourages kids to be the best that they can be. It's a friendly competition. Kids learn from and even cheer on their opponents. Odyssey of the Mind is not a competition about knowledge. It's all about creativity, an often overlooked element in the growth and development of many students. Kids are rewarded more for how they apply their knowledge, skills, and talents than for coming up with the right answer. In fact, here, there is never just one right answer.

What can children gain from Odyssey of the Mind? Kids learn at a young age skills that will last a lifetime:

- They work in teams, learning cooperation and respect for the ideas of others.
- They evaluate ideas and make decisions on their own, gaining greater self-confidence and increased self-esteem.
- They work within a budget, learning to manage their money.
- They see that there's often more than one way to solve a problem, and that sometimes the process is more important than the end result.

For more information on Odyssey of the Mind, go to www.odyssey-ofthemind.com

10

NATURE

Do the lyrics of Joni Mitchell's "Big Yellow Taxi" (http://www.jonimitchell.com/HitsTaxi70.html) resonate through your mind each time you see asphalt being poured? We definitely paved paradise to put up a parking lot. Our fondest childhood memories are set in the great outdoors—crafting snow angels, building sand castles, diving into piles of autumn leaves, chasing fireflies, and rolling on the grass with the family pup. How many of these memories will our children cherish now that we avoid playgrounds (fearing pedophiles), banish jungle gyms (worrying about litigation), and abandon the family pet (shunning allergies)? Waiting at the bus stop should not be a child's only contact with the great outdoors. Children have the essential need to experience and enjoy nature.

*****

Chelsea waddles from student to student, making sure she greets each and every one, despite the arthritis in her little old legs. Missy breaks from the crowd to draw in the shy girl who stands alone on the periphery. Bailey can't stop playing the clown, and Sweet Pea darts down the hall daring everyone to catch her, while Rosie plays ball with the new kids. They all love their jobs, and the students love them—a yorkie, a papillon, a beagle, a havenese, and a mixed breed. These and other four-legged therapists visit the campus to decrease stress, homesickness, and loneliness and to show the students how to have some good, old-fashioned fun. The students range in ages from seventeen to "mature adult," but all become children again when they "go to the dogs."

The benefits of animal-assisted therapy are well documented. Dogs, horses, and even dolphins aid the elderly, children with disabilities, and autistic children, just to name a few. But animals need not be certified therapists to help. Everyday companion animals lower blood pressure, ease stress, and relieve loneliness. A house is not a home without a pet or plant.

NATURE DEPRIVATION

For most of history, children were free to play outdoors in woodlands and near water. Two hundred years ago, most children spent their days surrounded by fields, farms, or the wilds of nature. By the late twentieth century, many children's environments became urbanized. But even then, and as recently as 1970, children still had access to nature and the world at large. They spent most of their playtime outdoors, using sidewalks, streets, and vacant lots or backyards, fields, and parks. Children were free to play, explore, and interact with their natural world with little restriction.

Today's children aren't so lucky. Their lives have shifted indoors, and outside play is minimized, as is their contact with the wonders of nature. The virtual world replaces the real world with nature channels and documentaries, conditioning children to believe that nature is something exotic in far away places they may never experience. Children are losing the understanding that nature exists in their own backyards and neighborhoods.

In his ground-breaking book, *Last Child In The Woods: Saving Our Children From Nature-deficit Disorder,* author and child advocate Richard Louv claims "Nature-deficit disorder" is making our kids depressed, distracted, and overweight. Children speak knowledgeably about the ozone layer and the vanishing rain forest, but many have little first-hand acquaintance with the flora and fauna outside their own doors. Far too many children have never climbed a tree, let a caterpillar crawl on them, or picked a dandelion bouquet.

Eighty percent of Americans live in urban areas that tend to lack park space. Asphalt and houses replace vacant lots in suburbia—a plight rapidly spreading to our rural areas, nature's last stronghold. Louv notes that many communities have virtually outlawed unstructured outdoor natural play, frequently because of litigation threats, but also because of a growing obsession with order. Some places require building permits for playhouses and tree houses, while other communities ban them altogether.

Unstructured outdoor play has been crowded out by structured activities and time spent in front of the techno-screens that abound in today's households. In fact, a study by the Kaiser Family Foundation shows American children spend forty-four hours a week glued to TVs, computers and video games. Louv quotes a San Diego fourth-grader as saying, "I like to play indoors better 'cause that's where all the electrical outlets are." But it's not only technology that keeps kids inside. It's also their parents' fears of traffic, strangers, Lyme disease and West Nile virus, and their schools' emphasis on more and more homework. Even organizations devoted to the outdoors now place legal and regulatory constraints on natural areas, sometimes actually making natural play a crime.

As children's connections to nature diminish, the social, psychological, and spiritual implications become apparent. New research shows that nature can be powerful therapy for such maladies as depression, obesity, and attention-deficit disorder. Environment-based education significantly improves standardized test scores and grade-point averages, stimulates creativity, and develops skills in problem solving, critical thinking, and decision making. Other research findings include the following:

- The impact of life stress is lower among rural children with high levels of nearby nature than among urban children with little nearby nature. Nature buffers the impact of life's stressors and helps children deal with adversity—the greater the nature exposure, the greater the benefits.
- Playing outdoors promotes running around, which helps children sleep better at night and battles the childhood obesity epidemic.
- Outdoor environments are important to the development of autonomy and independence.
- Children who regularly play in natural environments have more positive feelings about each other, show more advanced motor fitness, including coordination, balance, and agility, and get sick less often.

- Early experiences with nature are linked positively with the development of imagination and the sense of wonder, which are important motivators for lifelong learning.
- Children with attention-deficit hyperactivity disorder (ADHD) function better than usual after activities in green settings, and the greener a child's play area, the less severe his/her attention-deficit symptoms.
- Low-income children whose homes improved the most in terms of greenness following relocation tend to have higher levels of intellectual functioning following the move.
- Children who have contact with and views of nature score higher on tests of concentration and self-discipline. This exposure seems to improve their awareness, reasoning and observational skills.
- Playing in a more natural and diverse environment reduces or eliminates bullying.

NATURE AND NURTURE

Experiences with animals and nature may aid children in growing to be more nurturing adults. We traditionally think of children as recipients of nurturance from parents and other caregivers, not as nurturers themselves. Our culture places an emphasis on the individual, from our emphasis on individual liberties and privacy to our history of individual risk-taking through immigration to this country from other lands and to the West from the historic Eastern seaboard. As a result, Western child-rearing values tend to focus on the need to foster independence, initiative, and assertiveness. The need for children to care for others, to learn how to contribute to the well-being of others, is not well recognized by parents, educators, or healthcare providers. However, new research points to children's ability to nurture.

Most households have pets, and parents report acquiring pets because of the presumed benefits to their children. Interviews with parents and children indicate that pets generally assume great emotional significance, often being considered family members. Domestic animals and pets, as well as plants, depend on the care provided by the humans responsible for them. They signal their needs in fairly clear ways, and they provide rapid feedback when their needs are not met. Moreover, domestic animals and plants provide immediate and positive reinforcement when their needs are met. For children, as well as adults, experiencing the positive effects of your care on others may promote feelings of self-efficacy and positive connectedness—powerful reinforcers for nurturing. Nurturing animals and plants may be particularly beneficial for boys. In children's minds, caring for babies and young children becomes associated with "women's work" or "what mommies do" as early as age three, by age four or five, boys become less interested in infants and their care and even avoidant of baby-care experiences. However, there is no such association in children's minds when it comes to caring for pets or for plants, and no gender differences in behavior as children develop. Because pet care is "gender-neutral," it may be a useful training experience in the development of nurturance in boys.

GREEN IS GREAT—AT SCHOOL AND AT HOME

At school Fortunately, a growing movement in Western schools seeks to transform parts of their school yards from sterile areas of asphalt and woodchips with manmade equipment into naturalized environments that encourage exploration and play. The University of Scranton actually tore down a building to put in a green area! States including California, Florida, Maryland, New Hampshire, Utah, and Vermont, initiated greening programs. The natural school yards include mini-forests, ponds, streams, 'wild habitats', butterfly gardens, insects, animals, and gardening areas. Many programs use both place-based and project-based education to integrate their natural environments into their curriculums, making the schoolyards extensions of the classroom where hands-on experience with nature can take place during and outside of classroom time.

Research demonstrates the broad benefits of more natural schoolyards. Children learn by constructing their own knowledge, not by memorizing facts, and outdoor education fosters connected knowing, where education is part of life, rather than separate from it. The greater the diversity of natural landscapes, the greater the children's appreciation of nature and their experiences with it—schoolyards that are the most conducive to learning are those that are unstructured and not specifically designed for play. A study by the National Environmental Education and Training Foundation found that when schools use naturalized schoolyards in their instructional practices, academic performance improves in reading, mathematics, science, social studies, and writing. Other studies show a reduction in absenteeism and antisocial behavior, such as bullying, vandalism and violence.

At home   Get out and smell the roses—the petunias, evergreens, and fresh grass, too—and take your kids with you. Nature stimulates the imagination and engages all the senses. Look at all the plants, birds and animals, hear the songbirds and the rustling of the wind, smell the rain-freshened air, touch tree bark, and taste snowflakes. Nature gives you and your children a chance to bond, talk, and exercise, and it does not have to be time-consuming. A few minutes of a sunny day go a long way. They go a long way on cloudy, rainy, and snowy days, too.

- Go for a walk. Nature walks will enhance your child's appreciation of the natural environment. Ask him what he sees, hears and smells. Encourage him to touch, differentiating the roughness of bark from the smoothness of a rock. For young kids, this is science.
- Create a garden. Let your child pick what she wants to plant, or better yet, have her hunt for her own seeds. If you don't have a backyard, grow the garden in containers, on a windowsill or on the balcony.
- Make leaf masks. He can blend into the environment like a chameleon.
- Chase bubbles in the backyard.
- Watch clouds morph into animal shapes.
- Hunt for animal footprints and try to identify the animal that made them.
- Make and set up bird or bat houses.
- Skip stones across a pond.
- Go on a neighborhood safari.
- Make a rock garden with different stones.
- Roll over a log to see what's under it.
- Sing in the rain.
- Build a sundial.
- Make snow angels, snow people, an igloo or a snow fort—get creative and make your own snow sculptures.
- Wish upon a star.
- Find out how different animals and plants cope with winter.
- Do the daily bud watch and guess when the first bud of spring will appear.

Not too sure how to garden with your children? Try these suggestions from gardener Patti L. Mindock. Plant a simple pumpkin patch, or try a theme. Create a rainbow by alternating different colors of flowers in an arch shape. Plant a pizza garden with herbs and other necessary ingredients—oregano, basil, tomatoes, green peppers and onions. You can even plant it in a round plot with triangular sections that mimic the look of a pizza. Construct a bean teepee with tall metal poles (tied firmly together at the top) and lines of string between them. Plant bean plants so they wind their way up the poles and strings as they grow. Kids can go inside to pick their crop, munch the raw green beans and play in the shade. The type of garden you plant is limited only by your child's imagination (and the growing season, of course).

GET DIRTY

Now we go from nature-deficit disorder to dirt-deprivation. American kids are way too clean! Concerns about E. coli, pesticides, and lead poisoning now team up with fastidiousness to keep kids squeaky clean. How can kids be truly happy if they're never allowed to get dirty? Growing up in Yonkers, we had plenty of kids who weren't the cleanest on the block—but they certainly were some of the happiest, and they hardly ever got sick!

Kids love getting dirty. Left to their own devices outdoors, they're almost guaranteed to head for whatever's wet, slimy, muddy, or dirty. But today's kids are so dirt-deprived that there are websites and campaigns in both the US and Canada to encourage kids to get dirty! Baseball legend Cal Ripken, Jr., a big fan of getting dirty, teamed up with Whisk detergent to launch a crusade called "America Needs Dirt" (www.AmericaNeedsDirt.com). It serves as a resource for parents and caregivers on the benefits of outdoor play and getting dirty. Canada's Unilever Sunlight sponsors "Go ahead and get dirty" (www.goahead-get dirty.com), which has several outdoor related articles, including "Get Dirty U." Yes, both Whisk and Sunlight are detergents that benefit from dirt, but they're still promoting good, clean fun.

Getting dirty with your children can be very cathartic for you and a great way to connect with them. Dr. Dirt really knows how to dig up the dirt. He even has a recipe for Dirt Pudding (real food, not real dirt). Worried about your kid's digging up their own dirt? Have it tested. Contact your local health department or a nearby university for more information. Still turned off by the thought of real dirt? Use substitutes. Here are some down and dirty tricks:

- Sculpt in clay dough. Buy it or make your own. In a large microwaveable bowl, mix two cups of flour, one cup of salt, and tablespoons of cream of tartar. Add two cups of water and two tablespoons of baby oil. Stir well and microwave on high for four to five minutes. Stir again and microwave another minute. Continue to stir and microwave for a minute at a time until the dough is the consistency of mashed potatoes. Cool it to touch. Knead in your favorite food color. Store in an air-tight container or plastic bag.
- Fingerpaint—with your feet. Pour the paint onto paper plates and use your bare feet to create masterpieces on large sheets of craft paper.
- Get slimy. Buy slime or mix up your own batch. Pour one box of cornstarch into a large foil pan. Mix while adding small quantities of water. Stop adding water right when the powder dissolves. The mixture should be runny, between a solid and a liquid. Mix slowly. Add your favorite food colors for a fun effect. Clean up is a breeze; just add water, and the whole mess should wash away easily.
- Get all wet. Play water games in the family pool. Get out the water guns. Turn on the garden hose. Head to the waterpark.

Dirt is dynamite!

IMPORTANCE OF PETS IN CHILDREN'S LIVES

Pets serve as family members in the majority of American households, where nearly three-quarters of families with school-age children have at least one companion animal. Pets become a vital part of the healthy emotional development of children. As children develop, animals play different roles in helping children achieve tasks such as the acquisition of basic trust, compassion, empathy, and a sense of responsibility,

In a study that examined children's representations of support from their pets compared to support from human relationships, researchers found that pets were often ranked higher than certain kinds of human relationships, and they featured prominently as providers of comfort and support for self-esteem, and as confidantes for secrets. These results, developed from a population of twenty-two seven- to eight-year-olds, confirmed previous claims that pets may assume significant roles in children's social development.

Data was collected in another study on loneliness from thirty-two homeless youths, ages sixteen to twenty-three, who participated in focus groups. Findings showed that vulnerable homeless adolescents often recognized the therapeutic values of pets in terms of unconditional love, reduced feelings of loneliness, and improvement in their health status. For many of these children, the need to care for a dog excited their urge to act more responsibly and to make better choices, and for many, a dog was their only source of love.

In a review of professional literature, researchers Endenburg and Baarda described the effects of pets on child development. They note that caring for a pet aids in the development of self-esteem, responsibility, compassion and empathy forecast, as well as unconditional acceptance, social support, and (possibly) in the facilitation of language acquisition.

Companion animals are just plain interesting to children, sustaining their attention and stimulating their curiosity. Several studies of children ranging in ages from six months to six years showed that children prefer live animals, especially dogs, to motorized or stuffed ones. In one study researchers examined the reactions of two- to six-year-olds to a tarantula, an angora rabbit, a cockatiel, a golden retriever, and two realistic stuffed animals (a dog and a bird). The children ignored the stuffed animals, but responded to the live ones. More than two-thirds of the children talked to the bird, 74 percent touched the dog, and 21 percent kissed the dog.

KIDS AND PETS

Pets greatly enrich the lives of children. However, that enrichment should go both ways. Pets should be cared for—kept safe and happy in their homes. Don't get a pet if you don't have the time and money to care for it. No matter how much your child insists she will care for a pet, and no matter how old she is, some pet care almost always ends up as another of mom's chores, (whether the pet is a hamster, bird, cat, or dog). Pets require time, attention, and vet care.

If you're thinking of getting a dog, choose a breed that fits your family's lifestyle. Most purebreds were bred for a purpose (herding, hunting, lap sitting). Research your breeds of interest. Starting at the American Kennel Club's (AKC) website: www.akc.org. The AKC can also aid you in selecting reputable breeders. For cats, contact the Cat Fancier's Association (www.cfainc.org). Don't buy from a pet store. The dogs may be cute, but they are, too often, not bred by responsible breeders—good breeders want to know who's getting their pups! Pet store dogs usually come from puppy mills, and they may have health or behavioral problems (www.puppymills.com).

Better yet, go to your nearest animal shelter or rescue group. Rescue groups can be found at www.petfinder.org. Purebreds are available, but don't pass up the loveable mutts and adorable kitties! Shelter and rescue dogs can make wonderful pets. They're grateful to have that second chance at life, and they already have their initial vet care, including heartworm testing, vaccinations, spaying or neutering, and in most cases, a microchip for identification purposes should they get lost. You'll save a life, and your child will learn a valuable lesson about life.

Dogs and cats live a long time when properly cared for, so plan properly for that commitment. Responsible pet ownership makes life better for your family and your pet.

To provide a rewarding experience for your family and the pet:
- Recognize animals as living, feeling beings—they're not throw-away items.
- Decide when it's the right time to get a pet. Is your child ready for the responsibility of caring for the pet (particularly a dog)? If not, wait until he is ready. (Read the "Plants to Pets" section near the end of this chapter.)
- Realize that you, the adult, are still ultimately responsible for the well-being of the pet.
- Choose the pet that works best for your family:
    - Decide which species you want: Dog? Cat? Ferret? Other?
    - Realize that most dog breeds have been bred for a purpose: guarding, herding, hunting, lap sitting. Australian cattle dogs were bred to herd cattle by nipping at their ankles. If you choose one as a pet, the dog may herd your children in similar fashion. Border collies are the most intelligent of breeds, but they require considerable stimulation to prevent them from becoming bored and wrecking the house.
    - Read about the breed you're interest in to see if it is appropriate for children and your family lifestyle. What is the breed's typical temperament? How much time and energy do you have to devote to a pet? Some dogs require much more time than others for exercising and/or grooming. Some dogs shed; others need haircuts.
    - Puppies and kittens are cute, but they're also more active and more likely to bite. Your better choice is an older animal with a gentle disposition that was raised in a home

with children. If you do get a puppy or kitten, make sure it is at least six- to eight-weeks old.

- Provide your pet with appropriate nutrition, water, shelter, and love. Pets need socialization. If you intend to leave the dog chained outside all day with little or no human contact—don't get one! Besides being terribly unfair to the animal, its lack of socialization may lead to aggression.
- If required, get your pet licensed.
- Secure the services of a reputable veterinarian so that your pet can have lifelong medical care.
- Immunize your pet against rabies and other harmful diseases.
- Get your animal neutered or spayed. That makes him less likely to bite and roam, and it makes him healthier.
- Teach you dog basic obedience. If you're not sure how to do that, contact your local kennel club. The Petsmart (www.petsmart.com) chain provides basic obedience and puppy socialization classes at a reasonable cost. Dogs are pack animals, and they need to learn that you are the leader of the pack.
- Never leave pets alone with small children—no matter how well-behaved the children or pets are.
- Keep your pets safe. Don't leave them in parked cars on warm days—it can quickly turn fatal. Pet-proof your house. Prevent pet theft. Injuries to your pet will also be traumatic to your child. (For more pet safety tips, go to www.familysafety.com.)
- Keep your pet on a leash when in public.
- Teach your child to respect animals, and to never mistreat or hurt an animal.
- Tell your child not to bother an animal that is eating, drinking, sleeping or quietly playing with his toys.
- Tell your child never to take food, water, or toys away from an animal.
- Teach your child not to pet animals when they have babies (Of course, you'll have your pet spayed to avoid that problem in the first place!).
- Avoid rough play and wrestling with the puppy or dog as this encourages aggression.
- Cats love warm, soft places, so keep them away from cribs.
- Cats may also react aggressively to a newborn because a baby's cry is similar to other cats and small prey. Never leave your baby alone with the cat.

- Keep your cat's nails trimmed and dull to decrease injury (This will also reduced wear and tear on walls and furniture.)

If your baby arrives AFTER you already own a pet, follow these suggestions:

1. Allow your dog to investigate the new baby's room before you bring the baby home.
2. Practice leaving the animal outside the baby's room if the pet will not be allowed in once the baby arrives.
3. Bring home blankets with the baby's scent to get the pet used to the "smell."
4. Anticipate changes in your pet (increased barking, urinating outside the litter box) as a form of "sibling rivalry."
5. When you bring the baby home, allow your pet to sniff the baby's feet at a safe distance while leashed. Gradually introduce them to each other.
6. Never leave the baby alone with the pet.
7. Make sure you still give your pet adequate attention, and the two of them will probably grow to be best friends.
8. As your child grows, allow him to help care for the pet, (But keep small pet objects away from toddlers—they could choke on them.

If this sounds all like a lot of work… it is! But it's well worth it, if you can make the commitment. If you can't, don't feel bad. But do give your child plenty of opportunities to interact with animals. Take her to the zoo. Encourage your older children to volunteer at the shelter or to get jobs pet-sitting or walking dogs.

The following thoughts were specially prepared for *Let Kids Be Kids* by my friend, Jack S. C. Fong, M.D.

PLANTS TO PETS

By Jack S.C. Fong, MD

As integral components of the emotional and behavioral development of a child, the growing of a plant and the keeping of a pet are important commitments that parents may encourage their children to make. In caring for plants or pets, children will learn, experience, and master first-hand a number of very important life lessons.

While children are being parented, they will have opportunity to parent their plants and pets. If the needs of these plants and pets are not met, the outcome can be disastrous and regrettable. It is therefore highly recommended that the first preferred item is a plant. In the nurturing of this plant by a child, he/she will learn the power of observation, the value of assessment, the miracle of life, the science of biology, and the rigidity of biological needs.

Any failure in the growing of a plant by a child does not carry the high price of traumatic loss. Indeed, the experience gained from a failure should put the child to a better position to succeed when the initiative is restarted. Once the ability to care for a plant is demonstrated by a child, he/she may be promoted to the care of a goldfish. The experience will not only build on everything leaned during the growing of a plant, it will demand a higher degree of cognition, a firmer commitment to care, and some knowledge of marine biology.

From the successful keeping of a gold fish, a child may move on to look after a dog or a cat. The raising of a dog or cat is most demanding in the commitment of a child and family. The relationship is an interactive one with the pet assuming a significant emotional position in the family—often being considered as a member of the family. This acceptance of a pet animal into the family brings on an emotional connectedness with nature. The acts of caring for others, pleasure in companionship, and graciousness in giving are priceless foundations of self-esteem, happiness, and accomplishment.

The need to remain connected to nature is becoming more and more important as we, as a society, gravitate away from it. Humanity must accept the stewardship of our earth. Our children must learn about and get closer to nature if they are to be asked to value, sustain, respect, and preserve it. They may achieve this connectedness with nature by either spending time in the field or bringing plants and pets into their homes.

HEAVEN ON EARTH—GREEN CHIMNEYS

Founded in 1947, Green Chimneys is the nationally renowned, non-profit agency recognized as the leader in restoring possibilities for emotionally injured and at-risk children. Recognized as the worldwide leader in animal-assisted therapy, Green Chimneys operates residential treatment for children and a special-education school. Its mission is to help children reclaim their youth and the chance for a bright future through specialized treatment and educational and recreational services. Each year, Green Chimneys' restoration system gives hundreds of children and their families the tools that enable them to positively experience their youth, regain a sense of self-worth and create hope for the future as independent, positive, and productive adults.

Green Chimneys provides innovative and caring services for children, families and animals and targets its services at restoring and strengthening the emotional health and well-being of children and families—fostering optimal functioning and independence. They strive to develop a harmonious relationship between people, animals, plants, nature and the environment through an array of educational, recreational, vocational, and mental health services.

Today, the agency serves children and adults with handicapping conditions and regular children and adults from New York City, the mid-Hudson region, Westchester and Putnam counties, and the counties of western Connecticut. To date, the agency is considered the strongest and most diverse of its kind involving farm, animal, plant and wildlife assisted activities. For more information, go to www.greenchimneys.org.

11

UNSTRUCTURED PLAY

Play, especially, unstructured play, is critical for children's health. It increases peer interaction, releases tension, advances thinking, promotes exploration, and provides a safe place to explore potentially dangerous situations. It's also just plain fun. But today's hyper-stressed and overscheduled kids have less time and opportunity for unstructured play—even though they live in a time when they need it more than ever. We adults, must defend every child's essential need for unstructured play.

*****

Forty-plus years ago, my then three-year-old brother Joe begged Santa for "King Zor," a towering, two-foot animated dinosaur that came complete with a dart gun, darts, and yellow balls that Zor used as missiles. Flip the on-switch, and the big, blue Zor rolled about the floor, backing up and changing direction whenever obstacles blocked his way. Truly a wondrous site to three-year-old eyes in the sixties! Eager to help Kris Kringle, my parents scoured every toy store within a reasonable driving radius and finally found the elusive Zor.

On Christmas morning, mom and dad anxiously awaited Joe's reaction as he ripped off the wrapping paper. Joe was ecstatic, as were my parents, though mom and dad's ecstasy was short-lived. Zor spent his first three days lying lifeless by the Christmas tree, while Joe gleefully played with the cardboard box that had contained him—unstructured, imaginative play at it's finest!

To this day, the best gifts for tots include an old pot, a wooden spoon, a cardboard box, and the freedom of unstructured play.

PLAY AS A LOST ART FORM

Research indicates that playtime has dropped drastically in the last few decades, and an article in *Time* magazine comments that the very existence of research on play suggests that our serious society can rip the fun out of anything, including fun itself.

Studies by the University of Michigan show that children have lost twelve hours per week of free time since the late 1970s, including a 25 percent drop in play and a 50 percent drop in unstructured outdoor activities. Meanwhile, time spent in structured sports doubled, and homework increased dramatically. The amount of homework given to six- to eight-year-olds tripled between 1981 and 1997. This shift in kids' time created so much concern that it has given rise to the American Association for the Child's Right to Play, part of the International Play Association, whose sole purpose is to protect, preserve, and promote play as a fundamental right.

Kids can still have fun for the sake of having fun—kicking balls, running up slides, digging in sand, twirling in circles, laughing at nothing, and all the other blissful things that make childhood exhilarating. But now ball parks fill with organized games, parks run on empty, sandboxes turn to concrete, kids slump before TV sets, silence fills playgrounds, and recess fades into the past. Play is quickly becoming a lost art form.

Children rarely just "go outside to play" anymore. Instead they have play dates, take classes and lessons, or prep for sports. Kids spend inordinate amounts of time participating in organized activities, some squeezing in two or more before dinnertime. With every available minute filled, a child never learn how to deal with boredom or play on his own. Instead, he learns to be a miniature, schedule-juggling adult. Structured activities can certainly be beneficial, enhancing development and learning. But, too many parents believe that these activities are more important than unstructured play, which is seen to them as nothing more than a waste of time. So they banish free time and rob children of their personal creativity and imagination.

Driven by a plethora of twenty-first century fears, parents shield their children from everyday play. We worry that pedophiles lurk near every playground, that terrorists will strike our schoolyards, or that each grain of dirt contains flesh-eating bacteria. These fears may have some foundation in fact, but we have blown them out of proportion. We now fear fear itself—FDR is probably rolling in his grave.

Fun has also been pushed aside in the quest for higher standardized test scores. Young children face mountains of homework each night, and worse, more and more academic objectives are creeping into our preschools. And this persists, despite the well documented fact that play refreshes and stimulates the mind.

Technology serves as the final play assassin. Children sit motionless, glued to "flashy things"—televisions, computers, video games, DVDs, MP3s, iPods, camera phones, and other electronic gizmos. This passive form of play typically results in hours spent in doing little more than pushing buttons to activate electronic icons programmed by adults. TV bombards kids with so many commercials and product placement messages—what to buy, what to eat, what to wear, what to play—that children often feel they need to have the hyped props in order to play "successfully". They harass their parents into purchasing these licensed toys and then use them to mimic shows, engaging in scripted play—rather than unstructured and imaginative play. Since the deregulation of children's television in 1984, licensed toys have proliferated, accounting for at least half of new toys sold each year. (To make matters worse, many of the most popular shows linked to toys have violent themes that children often channel into their imaginative play through imitation.)

WHAT IS PLAY?

Mark Twain allegedly said it best. "Work is whatever a body has to do; play is whatever a body wants to do." Dr. John W. Santrock, author of the popular textbook, *Children*, says "Play is a pleasurable activity that is engaged in for its own sake." Two critical parts of this definition have faded: "pleasurable" and "for its own sake." Adult intrusion, time restraints, and rigidity suck all the pleasure out of play, giving new meaning to the old phrase, "play is the work of children."

How can we tell play from "not play"? It's sad that we have to ask what should be obvious, isn't it? But there are actually eight characteristics that identify an activity as play:

1. Play is intrinsically motivated. It's an activity done for its own sake. Motivation comes from within a child and involves satisfaction with the activity itself. Children make up their own goals and supply their own meaning to play activities, and these activities are not the result of external social demands or rewards.
2. Play focuses on the means not the ends. Kids at play focus on the play activities themselves, not outcomes.
3. Play contains an element of nonliterality or pretense. People describe pretend play by saying the child acts in an "as if" manner.
4. Play is pleasurable. Kids at play demonstrate joy, humor and happiness.
5. Play is flexible. Shifts in themes and materials occur easily and harmoniously.
6. Play is voluntary and spontaneous.
7. Children at play are actively involved, cognitively, physically, and emotionally.
8. Play entails "flow." Flow involves a centering of attention in which action and awareness merge to the point where children lose their self-consciousness and pay more attention to the task than to their own bodies.

These are mostly the characteristics of unstructured play. Unlike structured play, with its rules and identifiable courses of action, unstructured play is less specific and springs from point to point without set rules or objectives. Everyone contributes to the general idea without one child taking complete control. Twists and turns permeate this type of play and can keep the game going on for a long period of time. What may begin as a game of "house" can easily evolve into a quest for uncharted planets.

Unstructured play couples with heightened imagination to unleash unparalleled creativity, allowing children to be anyone they want and go anywhere they can envision. Through play, children better learn who they are and what they are good at. But these can only be accomplished if children have ample time to explore their interests, skills, and talents. Unstructured play allows for maximum exploration.

Structured play, such as organized sports and board games, requires adult-created rules to govern the player choices and identify courses of acceptable action. It's great for building skills and teaching children the importance of team work. Children enjoy these activities and have fun doing them, but structured play should not crowd out children's "free" playtime. Children who have their free time filled for them often have difficulty filling it for themselves when asked. Parents believe that all these extracurricular activities give their children an edge for success. However, they may actually be robbing them of the personal creativity and imagination that is needed for a winning lifestyle. Most highly successful adults can still adopt a playful attitude toward ideas.

BENEFITS OF PLAY

Still think unstructured play wastes valuable time? For all its fun and wonderment, play provides numerous benefits for children:

- A child's play expresses creativity, imagination, and initiative.
- It sharpens the senses, and builds self-esteem.
- Play teaches communication skills, and boosts intellectual and language development.
- It can involve exploration, investigation, and manipulation of the adult world.
- Play defines body boundaries and promotes mastery so that children feel in charge of their bodies.
- Play helps a child work off excess energy, and it helps in developing and improving muscular strength, coordination, and balance.
- Teaches cooperation, sharing, and healthy competition.
- Play can help a child organize life's discrepancies.
- It provides an opportunity to learn and practice leader and follower rules.
- Play allows for symbolic acting-out of painful physical and emotional states.
- Play can help develop the capacity to gratify oneself and to delay gratification.

Play and play contexts support intrinsic motivations driven by positive emotions. These emotions—including curiosity and awe—typically improve motivation and facilitate learning and performance by focusing a child's attention on the task at hand. Negative emotions, such as anxiety, depression, and stress, detract from motivation. Curiosity, flexibility, creativity, and insightfulness are major indicators of a child's intrinsic motivation to learn, which plays a large role in developing competency and personal control. Since play is intrinsically motivating, children perceive it as interesting, personally relevant, meaningful, and appropriate in terms of their abilities and their expectations of success.

HOW CHILDREN PLAY

Most of us have seen the joy on children's faces as they run through the sprinklers, play tea party, or toss a ball around the yard. But what lies under the play? How and why do children play? We now understand both structured and unstructured play, so let's dissect things even further by looking at how kids play at different ages.

NEWBORNS

It may be hard to imagine newborns at play, but all of their senses work to take in the sights, sounds, sensations, and scents of their world. They even get bored! Since parents comprise most of their neonate's universe, they become a critical part of their infant's play. Newborns fixate on their parent's faces and voices, finding this entertainment the ultimate in play. (Your face is your newborn's first toy!)

Newborns need lots of different things to look at, and most are riveted by the contrast of black and white. Flash cards and board books create great playthings, as do common household items suspended from the ceiling in at various distances and rotated frequently to give the baby something new to look at.

Fortunately, the world has yet to come up with soccer teams or ballet lessons for the newborn. However, some parents can't resist the call to fill their newborn's waking hours with classical paintings and French lessons. Don't let the stress on stimulating brain development make you feel guilty for every second your baby spends awake but alone. If you're too quick to formulate a play or educational module, you may actually interrupt the time your newborn needs to rest, gaze, process new stimuli, and just quietly play.

INFANTS

Babies spend more than half their time in exploratory or practice play. They play with their hands and feet, roll into various positions, and make fun sounds—rattling "raspberries" is a particular favorite.

During the first five months, play primarily involves visual exploration. Significant visual exploration can be noted as early as two months, and by four months infants respond to the meaning of visual stimuli. For example, babies prefer photos of human faces to other photos.

By five months, hand-eye coordination allows for guided exploration and the manipulation of objects by touching and mouthing. Tiny gums scan anything and everything that fits between the lips, so parents must make sure that dangerous items—poisons, medications, small objects, lead-based things, electrical wiring—stay out of a child's reach for at least the first three years.

Infants discover the unique properties of toys by seven months, usually choosing toys that provide positive feedback, such as busy boxes and play mats. By twelve months babies develop interest in how things work, becoming fascinated by light switches, push-buttons, and hinged lids on boxes.

Infants and toddlers experiment with bodily sensations and motor movements in sensorimotor play, such as the aforementioned mouthing. They play with repetitive movements. Baby drops a toy from the high chair. You pick it up. Baby drops it again. You pick it up. Baby drops it again. And again. And again. Sensorimotor play teams up with trial and error learning in this game—frustrating for you, great fun for baby. (This may have been the stimulus for inventing the yoyo.)

TODDLERS

Free play is big business for toddlers. They run, climb, roll, shriek, push things, pull things, and bang on things. As they play, they learn to manage their bodies, release emotional tension, channel aggression into acceptable behavior, become socialized, start to learn right from wrong, and discover themselves as individuals. Toddlers learn to have fun and to master skills.

During this stage, children have little interest in other kids except as a curiosity. Their play is solitary and may be parallel, meaning they play next to other children, but not with them. Toddlers play happily side by side, until one wants the other's toy. Then all hell breaks loose. Toddlers are unable to share and become distressed by the demands of sharing because they have a poorly defined sense of ownership.

By age two, toddlers love to imitate. They mirror adult behavior, playing games like setting the table, cooking, and flaunting early carpentry skills. Toddlers also love to imitate other toddlers. If one toddler starts banging cups together, others follow, adding their own unique spin to the activity.

Toddlers crave the experience of pleasant tactile sensations, particularly "squishing" things—clay, clay dough, finger paints, and mud. Squeamish parents beware! Depriving your child of this messy delight may result in him finding his own "squishing stuff," right inside his diaper.

PRESCHOOLERS

Preschoolers blast into play, intruding and bombarding others with purposeful or accidental physical attacks. They're loud, vigorous and consumed with curiosity. No one knows how to play as well as a preschooler!

Preschoolers enjoy rough-and-tumble play, or mock fighting, the playful, nonaggressive "rolling' around on the floor" that stays fun and typically does not result in injuries. Many adults discourage this type of play, fearful that it will result in future violence. But rough-and-tumble play is play (not real) fighting that releases energy and helps kids handle their feelings, control their impulses, and actually avoid inappropriate behaviors. (It also aids children in these times of touch deprivation.)

Dramatic play is the most important form of play at this stage. Preschoolers take on roles: playing house, school, and doctor; mimicking their parents; pretending to be a nurse, police officer, astronaut or builder. Unlike sheer imitation, this type of play also involves considerable fantasy and novel ways of interacting.

As many as 65 percent of preschoolers create imaginary playmates who become part of their regular activities. These characters are invisible friends who may seem quite real to the children who name them, mention them in conversations, and play with them. Invisible friends can be humans, animals, mystical/mythical creatures, or whatever young children can construct in their minds. They can be occasional visitors or daily companions. Some sleep in the children's rooms, some live in the walls, and many have their own chairs at the dinner tables across the country.

Imaginary friends provide companionship for periods of loneliness, keep secrets, provide reassurance and help children cope with fears. Children with imaginary playmates are more sociable, less shy, have more real friends, are more creative, and participate more in family activities than children without imaginary friends. Imaginary playmates seem to help children learn social skills and practice conversation, allowing them to play happily with peers and be cooperative and friendly with adults.

Imaginary friends may help children better master symbolic representation and the real world. They also aid in differentiating right from wrong, and blaming imaginary friends for wrong-doings usually indicates that a child can tell right from wrong but is not yet ready to assume responsibility for her actions. Finally, imaginary playmates can give valuable insight to children's feelings. When a child comforts her imaginary friend's fear of the dark or monsters, she tells us about her own fears and feelings in a way that makes perfect sense.

Parents and other adults should respect an imaginary friend—know his name, greet her when she makes her entrance, make sure not to squash it when sitting down (and apologize if you do). However, an imaginary friend should not be a child's only friend. Kids need to socialize with real children, too. Imaginary playmates should not shoulder the blame for all a child's wrong-doings, nor should they be pawns for adult manipulation to get a child to follow household rules.

SCHOOLAGERS

As children grow, their play develops specific rules and goals. They make decisions about taking turns, they set guidelines about what is and what is not permitted, and they enjoy situations where someone wins and someone loses. Tag and hide-and-seek pave the way for baseball and chess. Games develop thinking skill—learning rules, understanding cause and effect, and realizing the consequences of various actions. Language play develops into secret codes, tongue twisters, riddles, jokes, insults, chants, and rhymes. Dramatic play grows into the creation of secret clubs and participation in school plays. Fantasy play sneaks into the bedroom where schoolagers prefer to play in private with their miniatures, cars, and dolls.

From six to eight, children are chiefly interested in the present and their immediate surroundings. Since they know more about their own family, they play house and take on vocational roles they have seen. Although more interested in friends than parents, they occasionally enjoy having parents play their "child" or "student." This grants the child imaginary control over her parents, and it allows parents to understand how the child is interpreting them or how she perceives her teacher(s).

At this age, both sexes enjoy common activities, such as painting, making puzzles, flying kites, building models, skating, swimming, and rough-and-tumble play. A child imitates the roles of his own gender and becomes increasingly realistic in play.

By eight, children move on to more advanced models, collections, "how-to" books, farm sets, and trains. Loosely formed clubs with fluctuating rules pop up in boxes, basements, and tree houses. They enjoy the computer, but may also take pleasure in crafts, reading, playing instruments, or camping.

By ten, sex differences become pronounced. Through play each gender develops skills needed later in society, and this manifests through dramatizing real-life situations. From nine to twelve children develop more interest in sports, as well as in quiet activities. They love to improve their skills, enjoying things like carpentry, arts and crafts, needlepoint, music, dance, and photography—skills that can be short-lived when adults dismiss these activities as outdated, useless, or frivolous, (despite the tremendous self-satisfaction that can be gained from them).

ADOLESCENTS

An interesting thing happens when we move from childhood to adolescence, play changes into "leisure activity." We toss play aside to complete the transformation from child to rigid adult. Theorists actually argue as to whether or not true play exists in teens and adults. Thankfully, some theorize that playfulness is inherent in humans and that its manifestations just vary with life stages and culture.

Certain types of play—exploratory, constructive and dramatic—typically vanish by the teen years, creeping back only when teens help younger siblings, baby-sit, or act as camp counselors. Society considers these play forms childish (an adjective synonymous with death to teens). A type of dramatic play occurs when teens fantasize—dating the dream date, winning the big game, being a fashion model and—when they watch music videos or play fantasy games. This "playing around" with ideas (mental rehearsal) occurs into and throughout adulthood.

Teens engage in games with rules. These include board games, computer games and competitive sports. They horse around with rough-and-tumble activities—a nonthreatening way to rehearse relationships and have physical contact. Hobbies serve to break the monotony of day-to-day life and to provide a source of pride and accomplishment.

Most adolescents like to "hang out" at malls, parking lots, corners, friends' houses, and pretty much anywhere they can socialize in peace. Adolescents face a tough crossroad in life. Those who are not yet old enough to drive, to hold a job, or "to be taken seriously," frequently find themselves feeling as if they have no place to go. Thus, they look for places to hang out with friends who offer comfort, privacy and freedom—even though they tend to find their privacy in public places.

Their desire to spend time with friends, usually doing what looks like nothing, is overwhelming—and can be quite bewildering to parents. Though the comforts of home offer numerous amenities, teens still search for somewhere else to hang out. At home, parents too often blitz them with mom-and-dadisms. "All you do is sit around watching TV." "Don't you have anything to do?" "I'll need a surgeon to remove that phone from your ear." Feeling overly scrutinized, teens go off in search of nonjudgmental utopia. Let them be. You do need to guide your teens' social patterns, but you need to do so without a microscope.

RECESS OR RITALIN

We confine children to classrooms for almost eight hours a day, require them to perform in stressful situations, and then wonder why they're hyperactive? We strongly need to reevaluate our choice of Ritalin over recess.

Instead of working off stress by running around the schoolyard with friends, millions of children are confined to classrooms by policies that have cut or eliminated recess. This forces children to spend hour after hour in the classroom, even though union rules for most adult workers require a minimum fifteen minutes of break time for every four hours of work. The demise of recess and the apathy surrounding that development paint a gloomy portrait of contemporary America.

The reasons behind the recess recession run parallel to those that limit unstructured play. Some schools worry about potential liability issues related to playground injuries and dangerous strangers; others claim recess increases the incidence of bullying. However, experts claim that schools can prevent injuries, stranger danger, and bullying by properly training staff and students in both safety and anti-bullying measures. Other rationales for recess removal are early dismissal, utilizing recess time for gym, and the belief that children need adult leadership in order to be more productive.

The main reason for the elimination of recess remains academic. Schools want children to work harder to prepare for standardized testing, so they replace recess with more education. However, many experts say that this is counterproductive and that we place our children at an academic disadvantage when we fail to offer them time to unwind. Recess allows children to come back to class refreshed and better focused. Children in Finland get a 15-minute recess break after every 45-minute lesson, and Finnish children score at the top of international standardized tests.

The National Association of Early Childhood Specialists in the State Departments of Education (NAECS/SDE) takes the position that recess is an essential component of education and that preschool and elementary school children must have the opportunity to participate in regular periods of active, free play with other children. The NAECS/SDE further states that recess benefits children in four developmental domains:

- Social development proceeds rapidly during the early childhood years, and research strongly suggests that close relationships with friends contribute to both thinking and social development. Recess allows kids to interact with each other. During recess, children explore the art of expressing themselves to others, practice skills and rehearse behaviors—learning which behaviors result in approval or disapproval from their peers. They build cooperation, sharing, and conflict resolution skills, all the while developing self-discipline, a respect for the rules, and an appreciation for other people's cultures and beliefs.
- Recess aids in emotional development. It serves as an outlet for anxiety reduction, a means to manage stress, and a way to gain self-control. Kids learn about their own abilities, self-acceptance, responsibility, and perseverance.
- Recess provides opportunities to move and participate in physical activities, which in turn decreases restlessness and improves children's attentiveness. Movement is also critical for healthy growth and development, significantly decreasing children's risk for obesity, high blood pressure, heart disease and other illnesses. Active play allows children to learn about their bodies and practice the fine arts of running, jumping, chasing, climbing, batting, kicking, swinging, stretching and a host of things.

- Recess advances children's cognitive development: Research sub-stantiates the link between play and thinking. Simply put, children learn through play.

Playground play provides plenty of learning possibilities:
- Natural science—experiencing water, dirt, rocks, wind, and seasonal changes
- Wildlife—observing birds, squirrels, and chipmunks
- Physics—playing on slides, see-saws, swings, and merry-go-rounds
- Architecture—building with sand and blocks
- Math—counting and keeping score
- Language development—explaining the rules of a newly created game

To ensure that schools allow for recess and free-play periods, the NAECS/SDE recommends that parents, educators, policy makers, and others who work with children

1. support policies that require recess to be part of the school day,
2. back additional research on the benefits of recess and its effects on the four domains, and
3. develop policies and resources necessary to support aware-ness of the importance of recess and free play.

Children have the right to navigate their way across the monkey bars, negotiate a hopscotch course, tag their classmates, bounce a ball, and giggle for no reason at all.

WHERE PARENTS FIT IN

First and foremost—lighten up! If you spend hours reading Nietzsche to your fetus, teaching your two-year-old the theory of relativity, coaching your four-year-old for the SATs, or lining up early admission to Harvard for your six-year-old, YOU desperately need free-play time. Take a moment to swing to the moon, play jacks, or wonder if clouds are made from marshmallows or dryer lint. Play with your kids (but let them choose the activity). Lower your cortisol levels and be less serious.

If your child spends her day in school or day care, reduce or eliminate other organized activities. Limit her to no more than one lesson during the week and another on the weekend. She'll have more time for free play (and you'll save a fortune on gas and fees).

Minimize your child's screen time. Turn off the TV and send him out to play. Children spend an average of thirty-eight hours per week staring at the boob tube, exposed to sex, violence, and commercial values—things you'd normally ban from your home but have become oblivious to on the small screen. Limit computer use, and minimize the time spent on video games. Do realize that computer chat serves as free play for older children and teens, but it should not replace face-to-face social contact or interfere with daily living.

Choose toys wisely. Ignore her agonizing protests and refuse to purchase every licensed product known to child-kind. The drama will subside, almost as quickly as her interest (in the licensed toys she already owns) disappeared. Invest in free-time favorites—clay, paper, crayons, acorns, colored sand, pine cones, rocks, and lots of boxes. Stanley Greenspan, author of *Playground Politics* and *The Secure Child,* says, "The value of a toy is proportional to the degree that it invites imagination and creativity." Thus the value of a blob of Silly Putty® far outweighs the value of today's action-figure-of-the-week.

Let your child get bored. Boredom may forces him to read, be creative, use his imagination, and find other constructive ways to fill his free time. Boredom is a fact of life. It didn't kill you when you were young; it won't kill your child either—no matter how loud he whines. No matter what you do, you cannot eradicate boredom. It's here to stay. And learning to deal with boredom today can help keep your kids out of trouble tomorrow.

Sit back and watch your children play. You'll relax, reminisce, and learn more than you can ever imagine.

12

JOYFUL NOISE

They're rude, crude, and too often lewd. The bathroom language and disrespectful, careless demeanor of the "characters" who assault our senses during prime-time television shows are becoming imbedded in the behavior of our young people. "Gimme" and dead silence replace "please" and "thank you". Phrases like, "bite me" and "it sucks," as well as profanities, fill the air. Preschoolers talk back to adults. Middle-school kids bully vulnerable classmates with abusive and foul language. Children should sound like children, not like career criminals. They have an essential need to make a joyful noise.

*****

An attempt at casual conversation with the mother of a 4-year-old-or-so boy proved futile due to the child's troublesome antics. The child shrieked, cursed and pulled at his mom's pant leg as our elevator descended three floors to the lobby. Mom was oblivious to her son's behavior, never once attempting to address it, let alone curb it, even after I offered to help. My proposal was politely turned down with, "Oh, don't worry. He's like this all the time," as she ushered the youngster out the lobby door. My mind quickly fast forwarded to visions of what this child would be like at sixteen—and the image was not too pleasant.

Crudeness was once thought to be the domain of males, stereotypi-
cally those with questionable hygiene, big middles, torn muscle tees,
and the perpetual presence of a fisted beer can and stogie. However,
progress enabled crudeness to advance through the ranks, oblivious to
gender, background, dress-code and age. One study of students, ages
twelve to seventeen, found the use of expletives connected to social
power, especially among males, and the higher the status and power,
the more likely a child is to use "high intensity" language.

Far too many children behave poorly at home, in school, and in public. They talk back, liberally use profanity and crude language, or act
in a totally obnoxious manner. Rare are children who excuse themselves when necessary, use vocabularies laced more with English than
slang, and treat others with respect. Most children learn negative language right at home from the TV and/or from their parents, and they
start learning at a surprisingly young age. To make matters worse,
these behaviors have become so commonplace that we have become
apathetic to them.

KIDS AND LANGUAGE DEVELOPMENT

Human languages number in the thousands, yet there is no genetic
code that leads a child to speak English, Arabic, or Japanese. Language is learned. We are born with the capacity to make 40 sounds,
and we develop the ability to make associations between sounds and
objects, actions, or ideas. The combination of these capabilities allows
the creation of language. Though languages may sound very different,
all languages (except sign languages) have common characteristics:
They all have rules, all are made up of basic sounds, and all start with
the same sound—crying.

INFANTS

Language begins at birth with baby's first cry, the primary form of vocal
communication. Undifferentiated cries quickly give way to specific
ones that signal hunger, pain, a dirty diaper, the need to be picked-up,
and I-just-feel-like-crying. Cooing appears in a few weeks, becoming
very noticeable and controlled by two months. Vowels combine with
other sounds to create trills, and baby soon begins to chuckle and laugh.
Lolling—chains of vowel sounds—follows, along with pitch intona-
tions and single consonant sounds. By seven months, vowels plus con-
sonants equal babbling (mamamama, dadadada, bababab); positive

reinforcement of these sounds helps in mama, dada, and baba evolve into first words. Sound patterns become more complex from ten to twelve months when first words—commonly nouns—and "no" appear.

TODDLERS

Vocabulary grows slowly, but by age eighteen months most children know about thirty words. Young toddlers tend to speak in jargon—words that sound like meaningless gobbledy-gook. Typically understood only by parents and the toddlers themselves, jargon serves as a form of speech at this age. Vocabulary grows more rapidly after eighteen months, creating a spurt that grows into fifty to four hundred words by the time a child is two, although "no" remains a favorite. Toddlers also begin to put words together into two- or three-word sentences, such as, "me eat," and "mommy work."

PRESCHOOLERS

Vocabulary soars to fifteen hundred words by age four (twenty-one hundred by age five) and word preference switches from "no" to "why?" Preschoolers seek information, attention, and social acceptance by being inquisitive. Adult responses to their questions allow children to relate to others and solve problems. When they continuously fail to gain responses, preschoolers typically retreat into a fantasy world and neglect the verbal communication necessary for growth. Notorious for spouting all the family secrets, preschoolers love to exaggerate and tattle. Their egocentrism and limited understanding of the precise meanings of words frequently causes miscommunications, sometimes making them sound far more knowledgeable than they are, and triggering their experimenting with offensive language. Words that enter a preschooler's ears can roll out her mouth, and often at the most inopportune moments.

SCHOOL–AGERS

Language significantly expands from age six to age twelve. After age seven, children use compound and complex sentences and begin to understand the nuances of words. Chants, rituals and superstition demonstrate how intricately language and other aspects of development are interrelated ancient games and still permeate childhood: "London Bridge is falling down;" "Cross my heart and hope to die;" "Step on a crack and break the devil's back." These words hold a magical quality for children and are fun to say.

School–age language hosts distinct and unique personal and social functions. Language becomes part of the culture of childhood, a culture that is learned, shared, and transmitted among children, but that is received from and shaped by the adult world around them. Children teach each other the rhymes, chants, and rituals of childhood, and language enables them to master and control their expanding world.

Children begin to express humor through language during the school years. They delight in "knock-knock" jokes, puns, tongue twisters, riddles and goofy songs, like "Great Green Gobs of Greasy Grimy Gopher Guts," "The Worms Crawl in; The Worms Crawl Out," and the ever popular, "Diarrhea Song."

ADOLESCENTS

Advances in cognitive abilities in the teen years allow for increased understanding of language. They can give more complex definitions, frequently including all possible meanings or uses. They understand symbolism as metaphor, and figures of speech take on new meaning. They recognize the symbolism in verse and realize that the image conjured is a representation of something more intangible.

KIDS AND INAPPROPRIATE LANGUAGE

Young children acquire foul language pretty much the same way they learn other language skills—imitation. They dabble in gutter language as a normal part of development. They swear to be funny or to insult someone. When a parent frustrates their desires and things don't go the child's way, the child may express anger by calling the parent nasty names, even though the preschooler has no idea what the names mean.

Preschool cursing may be normal, but it's not acceptable. You need to correct this behavior before it becomes ingrained. Set an example, set limits, explain the hurtfulness of the bad words, and punish when necessary.

Older children use vulgar language for a number of reasons: to get attention, express anger, or exert power, to provoke or shock someone, to emphasize feelings, to fit in with or impress peers, to acquire social status, to gain control over a situation, or to relieve tension, frustration, or other uncomfortable emotions. If obscenities are tolerated or ignored, children often move on to other, more harmful acts such as open defiance or physical violence.

TV: FOUL LANGUAGE AND OTHER NEGATIVE BEHAVIORS

Compared to other media, TV demands attention by activating the nervous system with rapid movements and loud music. It centers on the brevity of sequences. Interactions between people and events are vivid and short, so its quick succession of material prevents children from actively reflecting on new content—in order to process or make sense of it. TV delivers information in short, fast-moving bits of imagery and talk to keep viewers' attention. Small children are fascinated by these images, but they don't have the thinking skills to understand them. Story techniques, such as flashbacks, close-ups, lighting and music are fine for adults, but they're confusing even for some middle school children who need help translating the story in a fast-paced program. Children miss quite a bit of what they see, often can't make connections, and are likely to focus on the more intense scenes—violence, sex, profanity—not the more important images, story elements, and themes.

Many families find TV situations, relationships, and story resolutions at odds with their own values, especially on issues of attitudes related to alcohol and drugs, sexual mores, violence and other criminal activity, and profanity. Without explanations or alternative models on how to handle life's problems, children quickly pick up TV program ideas as solutions. Consequences are not depicted, and children assume that certain actions have no repercussions.

Researchers Barbara Kaye and Barry Sapolsky examined the frequency and types of offensive language spoken on prime-time broadcast television, particularly on programs rated acceptable for children and teenagers. They found that the frequency of foul language during prime time TV jumped in 2001, after dipping in 1997, and that there was just as much profanity on shows airing at the eight o'clock [EST] family hour as those in the latest hour of prime time. Sapolsky noted that their initial work began in the early 1990's because of what they heard on prime-time shows: "Having grown up in the 1950s and the 1960s, I am still taken aback when I hear characters on TV using strong language that would have been absolutely forbidden in the 'old days.'" He points out that some sitcom adults use bad language even when speaking to children, citing an example from the "Bernie Mac Show," during which Uncle Bernie carries on about eating a "big ass doughnut." Nearly nine out of ten prime-time programs in 2001 contained profane words, even though most, like the examples above, were largely benign.

Swearing by television characters under twenty-one, through rare, was usually met with either a neutral or positive reaction on screen. Only one in ten incidents drew negative reactions on screen. The researchers' data suggests that swearing is most likely to be uttered humorously with the intent of drawing a laugh or positive reaction rather than to hurt somebody. However, Kaye and Sapolsky noted that these neutral or positive reactions—especially those involving children and young adults—may encourage viewers, including young ones, to use offensive language.

The increase in profanity may be significant, but it pales when compared to the surge in put-downs, back talk, and other disrespectful behaviors that seem to run 24/7. Negative role models abound. Courtroom judges insult plaintiffs, defendants and witnesses alike, while reality show judges do the same to struggling contestants. Obnoxious child characters spew put downs and disregard their parents every word. Overexposure to negative media can impact on the way children treat others, including their own parents.

HOME GROWN RUDENESS

Even the most courteous children act offensively at times. Most of them meet their downfall right at home, learning their wicked ways from their unsuspecting moms or dads. Recall the movie, *A Christmas Story*, when Ralphie Parker says the "f" word during the tire changing scene. Both his parents are shocked and clueless as to where he learned such a word, despite the fact that it appears to be his father's favorite.

Children who frequently use profanity, back talk and other obnoxious behaviors typically become teenagers who have trouble making friends and adults who make poor impressions. Their self-esteem dwindles as friends ignore them, and they have a tough time changing other's perspective of them once labeled rude and disrespectful.

Like the Parkers, most parents fail to realize how strongly their negative modeling affects children until it comes back to haunt them. Since we feel more comfortable to be ourselves when we're with those we love, we tend to say and do things we'd never do in public. This can easily lead to family dynamics that are impolite, rude and even offensive. Children see their parents barking commands, bossing and bickering. Worse, some hear their parents hurl hurtful insults and profanity at one another, being not only disrespectful, but abusive as well. Children mimic these behaviors and then run the continuum from insufferable classmate, to schoolyard bully, to domestically abusive adult.

THE LANGUAGE OF BULLIES

Children tease each other from time to time, calling each other names and engaging in horseplay. Teasing tends to be generally playful and humorous, commonly serving as part of children's social life with both parties sharing the fun. Bullying goes far beyond good-matured ribbing. It appears very similar to other forms of aggression, but with distinct features. Bullying behavior is purposeful, not accidental, with the goal of gaining control over another child, one who is physically or emotionally weaker, by using verbal or physical aggression. Bullies attack without any reason other than that the victim seems to be an easy target, and the result is intentional pain and distress for the victim.

Bullying usually consists of direct behaviors, such as taunting, threatening, hitting and stealing that are initiated by one or more students against one or more victims. Bullying can also be indirect, such as spreading vicious rumors that cause the victim to be socially isolated by intentional exclusion. Boys tend to use the more direct methods, while girls seem to prefer the indirect. However, be it direct or indirect, bullying is intimidation that occurs repeatedly over a period of time to create an ongoing pattern of harassment and abuse.

Verbal bullying use words to hurt or humiliate others. It includes name-calling, insulting, inappropriate jokes, swearing, making racist comments and constant teasing. Verbal bullying is the easiest to inflict on other children. It's quick and to the point and can occur in a short amount of time. The effects can be more devastating in some ways than physical bullying because there are no visible scars. The emotional scars, however, can be devastating, chiefly due to the relentless nature of bullying, a problem that remains constant from elementary school through high school. Victims of bullying report loss of confidence and self-esteem, anxiety, insomnia, depression, poor work performance, reluctance to go to school or work, social isolation, loss of friendships, the deterioration of personal relationships, and suicidal ideation.

CYBERBULLIES

Technology has created a whole new realm for verbal bullying—cyber bullying, the sending or posting of harmful or cruel text or images, using the Internet or other digital communication devices. Cyberbullying messages and images may be posted on personal Web sites or blogs, or transmitted via email, discussion groups, chat, Instant Messenger (IM), text and picture phones, and BlackBerries. Cyberbullies, mostly ages 9 to 14, use the anonymity of the Web to dispense pain without witnessing the consequences. Many cyberbullies are unrepentant, and their numbers are staggering, especially in affluent areas where technology is prominent.

According to Cyberbullying.org, the bullying techniques are as inventive as they are cruel:

- Sending cruel, vicious, and sometimes threatening messages.
- Creating web sites that have stories, cartoons, pictures, and jokes ridiculing others.
- Posting pictures of classmates online and asking students to rate them, with questions such "Who is the biggest __ (add a derogatory term)?"
- Posting unflattering photos of peers on the Web.
- Taking a picture of a person in the locker room using a digital phone camera and sending that picture to others.
- Altering pornographic photos by adding a peer's face to the image and sending it to porn sites or posting it in a blog.
- Breaking into an e-mail account and sending vicious or embarrassing material to others.
- Engaging someone in IM, tricking that person into revealing sensitive personal information, and forwarding that information to others.
- Criticizing or defaming teachers and administrators on the Web.

Cyberbullying may more harmful than traditional bullying because: 1) There is no escape; Cyberbullying runs 24/7. 2) The hurtful material can be globally distributed and is often irretrievable. 3) The bullies can be anonymous. 4) Children avoid telling their parents, fearing greater retribution, as well being forbidden to use the Internet.

Cyberbullying adds a modern spin to the rude, crude and lewd language of today's children. Technokids feel free to type whatever they want, no matter how disrespectful or cruel. Manners become virtually nonexistent in a virtually real world, and technology-impaired parents need to understand why.

According to Nancy Willard, the Director for the Center for Safe and Responsible Internet Use (CSRIU), several conditions foster online cruelty. First, the Internet (particularly blogging sites) serves as a vehicle for substantial self-disclosure. Teens post everything from sexual experiences to suicidal ideation. The more outlandish the posting, the more attention it receives—typically the primary goal of posting in the first place. Second, some cyberbullies claim they're exerting their right to free speech and claim this right as superior to all others. Third, the Internet creates what researchers coin, "disinhibition," which gives a sense of anonymity and invisibility to its users, and the [distorted value] of "I can't get caught, so I can do anything, and it must not be wrong." Teens act out alternate personalities online, thus they may instead opt for an "it wasn't me; it was my persona" excuse for bad behavior. Add this to the lack of tangible feedback, such as body language, in online conversations, and it's easy to see how this tangled web can dehumanize users, reducing empathy. Finally, social norms support the cyberbullying—"everyone does it."

RETURNING THE JOYFUL NOISE OF CHILDHOOD

Can we go back to a time when blackberries referred to fruit and children didn't even think about sexually harassing each other? We may not be able to alter technology, but we can bring back more civil behavior. To bring back the joyful noise of childhood:

1. Model positive language and behavior. If you do slip up while filing your taxes or changing a flat, admit your error and apologize for your negative language.
2. Instill good manners. Please, thank you and excuse me remain the basics of a polite vocabulary. Teach your children the magic words, reinforce them, and use them everyday. Coach children to ask for privileges, not demand them. The world will thank you later. Disallow whining, screaming and sarcasm; instead, encourage children to use an appropriate tone of voice. Insist that children use formal introductions when meeting new people, particularly adults who are not family members.

3. Racial, ethnic, and sexual slurs often sneak into children's language at an early age. Help them to understand that these words express prejudice and hate, and forbid their use.
4. Extend manners to telephone, Internet and other technology use.
5. Don't overreact, act shocked or get agitated when young children experiment with profanity. Calmly and firmly tell the child that others don't like it, and encourage your child to make up harmless or silly substitute words, like dang, sheet, shucks, and Mrs. Fletcher. Reinforce positive behaviors, and help your child discover new ways to express feelings.
6. Set household rules for avoiding fouls language and create consequences for when the rules are broken. Consequences should fit the crime—temporary removal of phone privileges for cursing over the phone, grounding for back talking a parent. Start a "profanity piggy bank." Require all household members to add money for each curse spoken, and keep a written record of who contributes. The person who contributes least, due to good behavior, wins the pot at the end of the month. Reward the whole family with a nonmonetary present if the jar remains empty for a said amount of time.
7. Counteract the negative aspects of TV:
   - Remove the TV set from children's bedrooms—permanently.
   - Don't use the TV as a baby-sitter.
   - Don't use TV as a reward or punishment. Both make TV more important to children.
   - Set limits on TV watching time.
   - Turn the TV off during conversations and meal time. Make family conversation time a priority.
   - Plan viewing together, in advance, by using your *TV GUIDE* or newspaper, and utilize the rating guides (L = coarse or crude language; D = suggestive dialogue, usually means talk about sex). Further information on ratings: http://www.parentstv.org/PTC/parentsguide/tvratings.html.
   - Preview programs first whenever possible. Screen new shows intended for children.
   - Forbid shows with foul language and heroes who behave badly.

- Use V-chip technology to block your child from watching inappropriate material on TV. Go to http://www.fcc.gov/vchip for further information.
- Use a foul language blocker such as the TV Guardian.
- Turn off the TV and provide alternate, more creative activities for free time.

8. Don't allow children to buy or watch/listen to movies, music, games, or videos labeled with parental warnings of offensive language.
9. When you watch a TV show or video that contains foul language, make sure children aren't in the room—or within earshot.
10. Promote the safe use of technology.
    - Keep the computer in a room that the whole family uses, and make the Internet a family activity.
    - Become computer literate so you can monitor properly. Check with your local schools or colleges for classes.
    - Discuss cyberbullying. Encourage your children to tell you if they are victimized, and make it clear that you will not tolerate their behaving badly.
    - Tell your children that you will periodically monitor their Internet usage and email, and do so, preferably in their presence. Sign on. Right click on your Windows Start button and click on Explore. Find your main hard drive (probably C), and look over the folders until you find History. Click it open to find out the sites your children visited. The site names are usually obvious, but if you're not sure about the content of one, double-click it to go to the site.
    - If your children become victims of cyberbullying, notify the school. If it persists, contact the police—some cyberbullying borders in cyberstalking.
11. Teach your children values: kindness, respect, courtesy, compassion.

Children should speak in the gentle and kind manner that makes them children. Let's put the joyful noise back into childhood.

13

YOUTHFUL INNOCENCE

There's no doubt that we'd all react with disgust at the mere thought of an adult sexually molesting a young child. Yet, far too many of us react with apathy at the ongoing sexualization of children in the US. The media bombards them with sexually suggestive material. Parents dress preschooler girls in seductive apparel, paint their faces, and coach them to parade flirtatiously in front of audiences to vie for coveted beauty queen titles. Predators solicit children online. Children are prostituted and trafficked. And, completing the cycle, children themselves become sexual offenders. Just how low can we go? Children have the essential need for youthful innocence.

*****

Despite seeing more than my share of troubled children over the past thirty years, someone always surprises—and disturbs—me. Such was the case of a twelve-year-old girl addicted to cybersex, who appeared on an episode of Judge Hatchett (www.judgehattchett.com). This girl admitted to chatting with up to 100 men per day, and having cybersex with at least 25 of them daily. During these virtual sexual encounters, she would use sexually charged language and, at times, flash her breasts via a web cam. When her mother found out, the girl stopped flashing, but instead sent nude photos of another female, as if they were of her. The girl phoned some of the men she met online, and eventually arranged to meet one. When questioned by Judge Hatchett, the girl had no idea of how dangerous any of this was. Judge Hatchett then did one of her famous "Reality Checks." (Her caring interventions really put her in a class by herself.) She sent the girl to the National Center for Missing and Exploited Children, where they discussed how other young girls were molested, and some killed, by men they met on the Internet. To cap the experience, they arranged for the girl to meet Skaterboy88, the "seventeen-year-old boy" the girl had planned to meet. When the girl opened the door, she was shocked to see a much older, big, burly man, who, fortunately, turned out to be a New York City Police Officer.

This is a frightening situation, one that definitely warrants starting the "Safety" chapter. But I chose to place it here for a reason. This blatant sexual activity, though "virtual," was performed by a child of twelve—a child who spends way too much time on the computer, and a child with sexual knowledge way beyond her years.

The sexual exploitation of children has become so commonplace that we often don't recognize it even when it's right under our noses. One in five children is sexually solicited on the Internet. Of the 70 percent of fifteen- to seventeen- year-olds who accidentally stumble across pornography online, 55 percent are not upset by it. Richard J. Estes, Professor of Social Work at the University of Pennsylvania, reports that between 244,000 and 325,000 American children are sexually exploited each year through child pornography and prostitution. He believes that "child sexual exploitation is the most hidden form of child abuse in the United States and North America today."

BEAUTIES AND THE BEAST

Unusually operated by for-profit organizations, beauty pageants are one of the fastest growing industries in the US, grossing over five billion dollars annually. The 1997 death of Jon Benet Ramsey catapulted child beauty contests into the public spotlight. This interest led to my viewing a one-hour special on these pageants that aired on one of the cable channels. At the end, my conclusions were: the pressure of competition was fierce, most of the girls lacked both the beauty and the talent one would expect to find in a pageant, and the mothers were spending high registration fees for the chance to win trophies that looked as if they were only worth a few bucks. While there are pageants that offer worthwhile prizes such as scholarships, one still has to wonder why parents would dress their child in a provocative manner and then parade her in front of an audience.

Hilary Levey, a 2002 graduate of Harvard, was curious, too. So she conducted a sociological study of pageants in Connecticut, Florida, and Massachusetts where girls, and some boys, between the ages of two and six competed against each other. Her findings demonstrate that the contests went beyond natural beauty and that the kids didn't choose to participate. They did what their parents told them to do.

Here are some aspects of these child pageants Hilary Levey found:
- Parents fit children with false teeth to mask lost baby teeth.
- Parents used fake hair additions if their daughter's hair was too short to curl.
- The children were asked about their "ambition/goal in life" (we're talking two- to six- year-olds here.)
- Parents spent between one hundred and two hundred dollars for pageant clothing—sometimes as much as a thousand dollars for a gown.
- Pageant fees cost between one hundred and two hundred dollars per contest, and the parents she interviewed averaged five contests per year.
- Some parents hire pageant "coaches."
- Each entrant gets some sort of crown or trophy simply for participating.
- One mother told her that some people have spent so much on pageants that they lost their trailers.
- Although pageants enforced norms of slenderness, the majority of pageant mothers were overweight.

One of Levey's most significant observations was the inappropriateness of the dresses, the "spectacle of little girls sashaying across the stage" in tons of make-up and clothing that make them look like Vegas showgirls instead of innocent children. Some performed sexy moves while in swimwear, while others wore special layered outfits that allowed each to rip off a jacket, then a skirt.

Revealing clothing and looking older often helps kids win pageants—but what do they lose? It's not difficult to see why many call this showcasing of young girls with lipstick, high heels, and provocative body language "soft-core kiddie porn"—which society tolerates and supports.

In his book, *Stealing Innocence: Corporate Culture's War on Children,* Henry Giroux shows how this competitive atmosphere imposes adult models on children, promotes restricted and problematic gender roles, and displays provocative sexual displays in young girls. Giroux focuses on the exploitation of children in "nymphet fantasies" in which adults project their desires and impose their models upon girls. His concern is with how children and youth are exploited and socialized by commercialism and the lack of public spaces and sites for the young to learn cooperative social relations and values in an increasingly commoditized and privatized culture and society.

In a Ball Sate University news report, the late Marcia Summers, former Chair of the Department of Educational Psychology, noted that these pageants may give children the perception that being pretty is the only option for success and popularity. They could pave the way for problems such as depression, anorexia and bulimia if these children cannot adjust in their teens. "We are denying some of these children their childhood," she reports.

MEDIA MADNESS

The US has one of the highest rates of teen pregnancy and the highest rate of teen sexually transmitted diseases in the industrialized world. Several factors affect early sexual activity, but the media—movies, television, magazines, advertisements, music and the Internet—are believed to play a major role. The media are the most easily accessible and remediable influences on young people and their sexual attitudes and behaviors.

A 2001 study, *Sex on TV* by the Kaiser Family Foundation, found that three out of four prime time shows contain sexual references. Situation comedies topped the list—84 percent contain sexual content. Of the shows with sexual content, only one in ten included references to safe sex, or the risks or responsibilities of sex. In those shows that portrayed teens in sexual situations, only 17 percent contained messages about safe and responsible sex.

Studies show that messages in TV shows, movies, and music have become more explicit in their sexual dialogue, lyrics, and behavior. These messages frequently contain unrealistic, inaccurate, and misleading information that teenagers take as fact. Teens rank the media second only to school sex education programs as their leading source of sex information. In one survey of 1,792 twelve- to seventeen-year-olds, researchers found that teens who spend more time watching TV with sexual content were more likely to kiss or make out, touch the breasts or genitals of a partner, or give or receive oral sex than were teens who didn't watch a lot of sexually explicit TV. Teens who watched explicit shows that promoted the risks of sex were less likely to participate in sexual activities other than intercourse.

Sexual themes increased in the lyrics of music and in the images of music videos. And at least one study showed a relationship between risky adolescent behaviors and a preference for heavy metal music. Soap operas, teen and preteen favorites, are ideal venues for sexual portrayals, and one study of fifty hours of daytime soaps found 156 acts of intercourse with only five references to safe sex (and unmarried lovers outnumber married ones three to one). Sexual themes, including bizarre ones, are common on talk shows, and even family-hour shows contain an average of more than eight sexual incidents, four times more than in 1976. Vulgar language is also increasing.

Sex sells, and commercials contain a tremendous amount of sexual imagery, including the inappropriate use of children in provocative poses. According to a report by the adolescent expert, Victor Strasburger, MD, sex is used to sell many common products, from shampoo to hotel rooms, but when children respond to these cues and become sexually active too young, people blame the children, not the advertisers. Heavy exposure to media sex increases the perception of the frequency of sexual activity in the real world.

INTERNET PEDOPHILES

Internet pedophiles are quite sophisticated in computer technology with some acting as entrepreneurs, selling products on their own home pages. Some predators gradually seduce children with attention, affection, kindness, and even gifts, sometimes spending considerable amounts of time and money in the process. They listen to children—empathizing with their problems and learning their interests and hobbies—and then gradually lower the children's inhibitions by introducing sexual content and context into their conversations. They build long-term relationships with children in chat rooms and even teach the children to manipulate their parents so that they "don't cause problems." Others immediately engage in sexually explicit conversations with children. Some collect and trade child pornography, while others seek face-to-face contact with children through online contacts. Computer sex offenders can be any age or either sex, and most don't fit the stereotype of the "dirty old man" in a trench coat.

According to the US Department of Justice Office for Victims of Crime, children and teenagers can and do become victims of Internet crimes. Predators can contact your children over the Internet and victimize them by: (1) tempting them through online contact for the purpose of engaging them in sexual acts; (2) using the Internet for the production, manufacture, and distribution of child pornography; (3) using the Internet to expose your children to child pornography, and encouraging them to exchange pornography; and (4) enticing and exploiting your children for the purpose of sexual tourism (travel with the intent to engage in sexual behavior) for commercial gain and/or personal gratification.

The US Department of Justice Office for Crime Victims notes that there are several characteristics that distinguish Internet crimes from other crimes committed against children. Actual physical contact between the child and the perpetrator doesn't need to occur for a child to be a victim or for a crime to be committed. Innocent pictures can be digitally transformed into pornographic material and distributed across the Internet without the victims' knowledge.

The Internet provides a source for long-term victimization of a child that can last for years, often without the victim's knowledge. Once a pornographic photo of a child is displayed on the Internet, it can stay there forever without damage to the quality of the image. Internet child abuse transcends jurisdictional boundaries, frequently involving multiple victims from different communities, states, and countries. The geographic location of a child is not a major concern for perpetrators who target victims over the Internet. Pedophiles often travel hundreds of miles to engage in sexual acts with children they met over the Internet. Many child victims of Internet crimes don't reveal their victimization or even realize that they have been victims of a crime. Many victims of Internet crimes remain anonymous until pictures or images are discovered by law enforcement during an investigation. The presumed anonymity of Internet activities often provides a false sense of security and secrecy for both the victim and the perpetrator.

Children, particularly teens, can be very curious about sex and sexually explicit material. They may be seeking more independence from their parents and looking to develop new relationships outside the family. The Internet acts as an easy tool for these children—they can search pornographic material in the privacy of their computer for free without having to worry about nosey adults supervising them at the magazine stand. Pedophiles are well aware of this, and they use the children's curiosity to lure them in.

The Internet is an exciting and helpful tool, but it can also be very dangerous. Therefore you need to take steps to keep your children safe. Don't assume that they'll be protected by the supervision or regulation of the online services.

Use the following guidelines to help keep your child safe:

- Keep the computer in a room that the whole family uses, and make the Internet a family activity. This way you can keep an eye on him. Tell him he can't do anything on-line unless you can see what he's doing.
- Become computer literate so you can monitor your child properly. Check with your local schools or colleges for classes.
- Discuss sexual victimization and Internet dangers. Talk to her about the issues that concern you, such as violence, pornography, hate literature, and exploitation. This way she'll know how to respond should she encounter these things.
- Use blocking or filtering software to allow you to control your children's access to certain areas on the Internet. Different products offer various levels of parental control, so investigate each one carefully to choose the one best for your family.
- Be aware that your children can outsmart many of the parental controls and filtering services. Therefore, nothing can replace your supervision and involvement.
- Limit the amount of time she spends online. You can print out a "Family Contract for Online Safety" for you and your child to sign at www.SafeKids.com—a site devoted to online and technology safety.
- Establish clear and concise rules for using the computer, and post them near the computer.
- Keep tabs on your child's Internet usage. If he suddenly logs off when you enter the room, or you suspect that he may be doing something inappropriate, find their history trail. Sign on to your service provider. Right click on your Windows Start button and click on Explore. Find your main hard drive (probably C), and look over the folders until you find History. Click it open to

find out the sites your child has visited. The site names are usually obvious, but if you're not sure about the content of one, double-click it to go to the site.

- Purchase tracking software to track where your child goes online. These programs allow you to monitor the length of time she spends on the Internet, time of day sites were visited, sites visited, and time spent offline but on the computer. One example is Spector Pro, by SpectorSoft (www.spectorsoft.com), that records e-mails, chats, instant messages, keystrokes and websites, and provides screen snapshots, Internet blocking, and danger alerts.
- Randomly check your child's e-mail, but remember that he may be contacted via the US mail, too. Be honest about your access so as not to lose his trust.
- Find out what Internet safeguards are used by your child's school, her friends, and the library. These are areas outside your supervision where she may encounter an online predator.
- The FBI suggests that you teach your child to:

  1) Never arrange a face-to-face meeting with a person she met online.
  2) Never post photos of himself on the Internet or e-mail them to people he doesn't personally know.
  3) Never give out her name, address, phone number, e-mail address, or any other identifying information.
  4) Never download anything from an unknown site or e-mail as it may contain sexually explicit or other objectionable information.
  5) Never respond to suggestive, obscene, harassing, or belligerent messages or postings.
  6) Realize that what he reads online may or may not be true.
  7) Always tell you when an online experience makes her uncomfortable.

CHILD PORNOGRAPHY

The FBI's National Incidence-Based Reporting System (NIBRS) data from 1997 to 2000 revealed that the proportion of child pornography increased from 15 percent in 1997 to 26 percent in 2000—an important statistic given that this increase occurred in the context of an overall decline in reported cases of child sexual abuse and sex crimes in general. "Lone adult" offenders committed the most offenses, and victims were described as: 65 percent female, 25 percent members of the offender's family, 59 percent were teens (twelve to seventeen years), 28 percent were elementary school children (six to eleven years), and 13 percent were preschoolers (younger than six years). Legal definitions of child pornography vary from state to state and under federal law, but most definitions involve a visual depiction (not the written word) of a child that is sexually explicit. In contrast to adult pornography, but consistent with the gender preference of many pedophiles, there is a high percentage of child pornography depicting boys.

Because child pornography was once hard to obtain, some pedophiles have or had only child erotica in their collections. (Child erotica has been defined as visual images of children or naked children that are not considered pornographic, as well as any material, relating to children, that serves a sexual purpose for a given individual.) However, computers and the Internet now make child pornography more readily available. Child pornography is so quickly available on the Internet—it's possible to store a collection in cyberspace and download it anytime.

Researchers Kenneth Lanning, Carol R. Hartman, and Ann W. Burgess identified four kinds of child-pornography collectors: (1) The closet collector keeps his collection a secret and is not actively involved in molesting children. (2) The isolated collector actively collects porn and molests children. His collection may include photos of his victims taken by him and other material. (3) The cottage collector shares his collection and (evidence of his sexual activity) with others, usually to validate his behavior. Money or profit is not a significant motivating factor. (4) The commercial collector acknowledges the monetary value of his collection and sells duplicates to other collectors. Although profit is important, these offenders are usually active sexual molesters themselves.

Child pornography can be either commercial or homemade. Commercial child pornography is produced and intended for commercial sale. Because of strict laws, commercial child pornography is not openly sold in the US currently. Some commercial child pornography being distributed in the United States was smuggled in from foreign countries by pedophiles. Commercial child pornography is more readily available in foreign countries, but US citizens seem be the main customers for much of this material. Contrary to what its name implies, homemade child pornography can be as good as, if not better than, any commercial pornography, primarily because the pedophile has a personal interest in the product. Homemade simply means it was not originally produced for sale. Rarely found in "adult" bookstores, child pornography is too frequently found in the homes and offices—especially on the computers—of doctors, lawyers, teachers, scout leaders, clergy members, and other apparent pillars of the community. Although not openly sold in stores anywhere in this country, homemade child pornography is continually produced, swapped, and traded in almost every community in the US, primarily via the Internet.

Two subcategories of child pornography are technical child pornography and simulated child pornography. The federal child pornography laws define a child as anyone younger than the age of eighteen. Thus a sexually explicit photograph of a pubescent, mature-looking fifteen- to seventeen-year-old girl or boy is called technical child pornography. It doesn't look like child pornography, but it is. Technical child pornography is an exception to much of what is said about child pornography—it often is produced, distributed, and consumed by individuals who are not child molesters. It is more openly sold in stores and distributed around the United States. It more often portrays females than males. In essence, because it looks like adult pornography, it is treated more like adult pornography. Simulated child pornography consists of sexually explicit photographs of eighteen-year-olds or older adults made up to look youthful. It is not legally child pornography, but the material could be of interest to pedophiles.

More than twenty thousand images of child pornography are posted on the Internet every week, and more than half of the illegal websites are hosted in the US. The typical age of the children involved is six to twelve, but the demand for infant and toddler pornography is soaring. Because of the reach of the Internet, cybersex offenders are particularly threatening to the community. From the safety of their homes, pedophiles can use the web to anonymously and simultaneously prepare numerous children for future molestations. With one click of the mouse, they can easily distribute their collections to many other offenders, or even to juveniles.

Pedophiles who target young people use computers for purposes that may include viewing, storing, producing, sending, and receiving child pornography, contacting, grooming, and enticing juveniles for victimization, and communicating with—and thus, helping to validate—each other. Before the Internet, individuals with deviant tendencies were usually isolated. Now offenders feel normal because they see from chat rooms and websites that many other individuals have the same interests. This reinforces their behavior, perhaps emboldening them to commit acts, such as sex with a child, in the real world. According to the FBI, once arrested, these individuals often will attempt to justify their actions: "I downloaded them by accident. I did not know it was child pornography. It was just fantasy. I never intended to have sex with a minor. I just had dirty pictures. I did not hurt anyone. A hacker put these files on my computer. I have them so I will not abuse children."

The FBI notes that a cybersex offender finds the Internet a compelling tool for his deviant behavior for four general reasons:

1. The Internet provides anonymity. He can communicate with whomever he wants with little fear of discovery. Furthermore, he can portray anyone—someone of the opposite sex, single, more attractive, less overweight, or similar in age to the victim—in his attempts to entice juveniles online.
2. Using the Internet, a sex offender can groom multiple victims over an extended period of time and simultaneously—something that would prove harder and riskier to accomplish in the real world.
3. Digital equipment greatly enhances the ability to store, catalog, and retrieve his collection. His computer can maintain thousands of pornographic files, hidden from his family members and employer, yet readily available for viewing and other purposes.
4. Advanced technology permits anyone to produce pornography. A Pedophile can easily morph innocuous pictures into explicit ones and even put himself into the picture. He can also take digital photos of his victims without worrying about the risks associated with having the film developed.

Through the Internet, an offender can affect victims without any physical contact. He can easily forward explicit images to juveniles. The offender uses electronic images of child pornography and even favorite cartoon characters engaged in sexual acts to encourage juveniles to participate in inappropriate conduct. This exposure desensitizes young people and makes them think such behavior is normal. An offender can also obtain innocent pictures of children via the Internet or other sources and then morph those images into pornography. These juveniles and their families may not become aware of this type of victimization until the photos begin surfacing online. For these victims, finding justice can prove difficult. No one country or authority governs the Internet's content, so issues of child pornography and exploitation frequently cross jurisdictional boundaries. This causes not only legal problems but also difficulties for juveniles and their families when seeking remedy.

The children used in pornography are desensitized and conditioned to respond as sexual objects. They are frequently ashamed and must deal with the permanency, longevity, and circulation of such a record of their sexual victimization. Some forms of sexual activity can be repressed and hidden from public knowledge. When this occurs, child victims can hope that some day the activity will be over, so they can make a fresh start. Many children, especially teen boys, fervently deny their involvement with a pedophile—but there is no denying or hiding from a sexually explicit photograph or videotape. That child in a photograph, video or website is young forever, and the material can be used over and over again for years. Some victims have even committed crimes attempting to retrieve or destroy the permanent records of their molestation.

THE PROSTITUTION OF CHILDREN

The prostitution of children takes place in a variety of circumstances. International and interstate criminal organizations traffic young girls with promises of employment and money. Parents prostitute their children over the Internet. Homeless, throwaway, and runaway kids engage in survival sex, often lured into prostitution by sophisticated criminals who convince them they will be taken care of and will have the secure, loving environment that they lacked at home. But pimps breach their promises, taking the money a child earns on the streets and engaging in severe physical abuse to build a relationship of dependency. Drug dealers force addicted teens to prostitute themselves to receive drugs or a place to stay. Gangs require members to engage in sex for money or other services as part of initiation rights. And middle-class youths, acting on their own or with friends, prostitute themselves for money and adventure.

Juvenile prostitution has similarities to and differences from adult prostitution. Both offender groups are predominantly white. Both tend to encounter police in the evening, and both groups are more active in the warmer weather. However, unlike their adult counterparts, juvenile prostitutes are more likely to be male and are more likely to be encountered in multiple offender groups. Most juvenile prostitution incidents take place outdoors (highways, roads, alleys, woods, parking lots), as well as in homes and residences.

A recent study by Richard Estes of the University of Pennsylvania shows that child sexual exploitation affects as many boys as girls, but that boys are less well served by human services and law enforcement systems because of the belief that boys can fend for themselves. However, boys exhibit higher levels of emotional problems, drug abuse and violence, and many shift from being victims of sexual abuse to victimizing other boys and girls as pimps and traffickers.

Urban street children are not the only ones prostituting themselves. Middle class kids get involved in prostitution, as well as pornography, to earn money for luxury goods. Some engage in commercial sex while living in secure middle-class homes, and few parents are aware of their children's involvement in pornography or prostitution. Most of their customers are members of their own junior and senior high school peer groups.

TRAFFICKING AND TOURISM

Sex trafficking and sex tourism are monstrous crimes that victimize the most vulnerable among us. Trafficking is a modern-day form of slavery. Traffickers often prey on the poor and those who may lack access to social safety nets, predominantly women and children. They lure victims with false promises of good jobs and better lives, and then force them to work under brutal and inhuman conditions or use them for sexual exploitation.

When an offender takes a woman or girl against her will and forces her to engage in prostitution, that offender has stolen her freedom and her dignity. Much trafficking is international, with victims being taken from places such as South and Southeast Asia, the former Soviet Union, Central and South America, and other less-developed areas.

Many are brought or sent to more developed places including Asia, the Middle East, Western Europe, and North America.

Unfortunately, the United States not only faces an influx of international victims of sex trafficking, but it also has its own homegrown problem of interstate sex trafficking of minors. The interstate sex trafficking of minors is a growing problem. The Estes report estimated that about 293,000 American youth are currently at risk of becoming victims of commercial sexual exploitation. Most are either runaways or throwaways and live on the streets.

Other children are recruited into prostitution through forced abduction, pressure from parents, or through deceptive agreements between parents and traffickers. Once these youths become involved in prostitution, they are often forced to travel far from their homes, resulting in isolation from their friends and families. Few children are able to develop new relationships with peers or adults outside their role as victims of violence, forced drug use, and constant threats.

Approximately 55 percent of street girls engage in formal prostitution. Of the girls engaged in formal prostitution, about 75 percent work in pimp-controlled commercial sexual exploitation linked to escort and massage services, private dancing, drinking and photographic clubs, major sporting and recreational events, major cultural events, conventions, and tourist destinations. About 20 percent of these children become entangled in nationally organized crime and are trafficked nationally. They are transported around the US by cars, buses, vans, trucks or planes, and are often provided counterfeit identification to use in the event of arrest. The average age at which girls first become victims of prostitution is twelve to fourteen; for boys and transgender youth, the average age of entry into prostitution is eleven to thirteen.

Sexual tourism is one of the largest, most lucrative industries worldwide. For many vacationers, particularly those traveling from industrialized nations to developing countries, paying for sex is an integral part of the travel experience. Each year foreign travelers from predominantly Western countries pump billions of dollars into the economies of developing nations when they purchase sexual services.

Children are frequently targeted by travelers for commercial sexual exploitation. The United Nations defined child sex tourism as "tourism organized with the primary purpose of facilitating the effecting of a commercial sexual relationship with a child." Child advocacy groups identify three major categories of sexual exploitation of minors for monetary gain: prostitution, pornography, and trafficking for sexual purposes.

A common myth about molesters is that they're all pedophiles. Although pedophiles contribute to the problem, the majority of customers who pay money to sexually exploit children are first and foremost prostitute users. These customers, who come from all walks of life, may or may not actively seek out underage victims, and their use of sex workers may be habitual or situational. Most are males from wealthy, industrialized nations like the United States, Germany, the United Kingdom, Australia, France, and Japan (also called "sending countries").

Children are sought out for a variety of reasons. In many countries, virgins are at a premium because they are prized for their youth, purity, and expected lack of sexually transmitted diseases. Some sex tourists prize the innocence of children, while others correlate youth with beauty or attractiveness. Some choose minors due to a racist ideology that views children from other cultures as more highly sexualized than those in the West and perceives sex with children in foreign cultures as being "natural." Others justify their actions as being financially beneficial for destitute children. Finally, some sex tourists do not claim to choose youth. They generally deny that the person they were sexually involved with was underage and renounce any kind of moral complicity for the perpetuation of the child sex industry.

JUVENILE SEX OFFENDERS

The sexualization of youth comes full circle—they have now become the abusers. It's estimated that juveniles account for up to one-fifth of the rapes and one-half of the child molestation cases committed in the US each year. The majority of cases appear to involve adolescent male perpetrators. However, a number of studies have demonstrated the presence of females and prepubescent youths who have engaged in sexually abusive behaviors.

A number of casual influences have been identified to help explain the development of juvenile sex offenders. The most prominent factors include maltreatment, exposure to pornography, substance abuse, and exposure to aggressive role models. However, little research has been done on the subject of juvenile sex offenders. Juveniles who have committed sex offenses are a mixed group. They vary according to victim and offense characteristics and a wide range of other variables, including types of offending behaviors, histories of maltreatment, sexual knowledge and experiences, academic and cognitive functioning, and mental health problems.

John Hunter, of the Juvenile Forensic Evaluation Resource Center, noted that juvenile offenders appear to fall into two major types—those who offend against peers or adults, and those who target children. He summarized their differences and similarities:

Juvenile offenders who sexually offend against peers or adults:
- predominantly assault females and strangers or casual acquaintances;
- usually commit their assaults in association with other types of criminal activity (e.g., burglary);
- usually have histories of non-sexual criminal offenses, and appear more generally delinquent and conduct disordered;
- tend to commit their offenses in public areas;
- generally display higher levels of aggression and violence in the commission of their sexual crimes; and
- frequently use weapons to cause injuries to their victims.

Juvenile offenders who sexually offend against children:
- have at least one male victim (50 percent of this group);
- count as many as 40 percent of their victims as siblings or other relatives;
- tend to have crimes more of opportunity and guile than injurious force (may trick the child into complying with the molestation, use bribes, or threaten the child with loss of the relationship);
- may display high levels of aggression and violence;
- have often been characterized as suffering from deficits in self-esteem and social competency; and
- show evidence of depression.

Characteristics common to both groups of juvenile sex offenders include:
- high rates of learning disabilities and academic dysfunction (30-60 percent);
- other behavioral health problems, including substance abuse and disorders of conduct (up to 80 percent have some diagnosable psychiatric disorder);
- difficulties with impulse control and judgment.

FEMALE JUVENILE OFFENDERS

Research on girls who have committed sex offenses has been relatively rare, but recent studies have found an increase in their numbers. The incidence may be underestimated because of societal unwilling-ness—and even reluctance among professionals—to acknowledge that girls are capable of committing such offenses.

Female offenders tend to be younger than the males and are less likely to have perpetrated acts of rape. The girls are more likely to be victims of sexual abuse, and are more likely to have experienced multiple types of abuse. Most adolescent girls who have sexually victimized young children did so while engaged in a childcare situation. A study that compared sixty-seven girls and seventy boys who had histories as sex offenders found meaningful similarities and differences. The girls' reported behaviors were similar to the boys' in types of offenses committed, and both tended to victimize young children of the opposite gender. But girls typically had more severe victimization experiences themselves.

CHILD SEX OFFENDERS

The percent of children under age thirteen arrested for forcible rape grew from 4 percent in 1980 to 12 percent in 1997, and the rate of arrests for other sexual offenses rose from 11 percent to 19 percent in the same time period. Research in the area of prepubertal sex offenders is still in its infancy, but professional literature reveals that some children are sexually aggressive as early as age three or four, although the most common age of onset appears to be between six and nine. Contrary to findings regarding adolescent sex offenders, girls were represented in much greater numbers among preadolescent offenders. Furthermore, these girls often engaged in behaviors that were just as aggressive as the boys' actions. Victims of child sex offenders range in ages from one to nine, and many offenders have multiple victims. Victims tend to be quite vulnerable and are typically siblings, friends, or acquaintances, and most often, female.

Clinical observations have long suggested that many young sex offenders were sexually victimized before they began offending, and rates of victimization appear to be even higher in prepubescent offenders. Other contributing factors include: physical abuse, a history of impaired family functioning, self-esteem and social skill deficits, poor impulse control, psychopathology, lack of empathy, and deviant sexual interests.

PREVENTING CHILD AND ADOLESCENT SEXUAL EXPLOITATION

The problem of childhood sexualization is horrific, and it will not go away unless we do something about it. We must protect children.

The National Center for Missing and Exploited Children and the Office of Juvenile Justice and Delinquency Prevention have developed guidelines for parents, schools, and communities to reduce the incidence of sexual exploitation. I have combined and modified theirs to compose the following guidelines:

Parents should make strong habits of these behaviors:
- Pay attention when your child tells you he doesn't want to go with someone or to a particular place.
- Keep the lines of communication open.
- Notice if someone is paying too much attention to your child.
- Teach your child she has the right to say "NO!" to unwelcome or uncomfortable actions or touches.
- Be alert for changes in your child's behavior. Look for small clues that may mean he's in trouble.
- If your child confides in you, remain calm and nonjudgmental.
- Screen babysitters and other caregivers. Check references and run background checks if possible—check with your state police.
- Know what your child is doing—including her Internet activity.
- Be involved in your child's life.
- Make sure your child's school has a safety program.
- Practice basic safety skills.
- Don't 'hypersexualize' your child—she'll grow up fast enough on her own.

School officials and/or teachers should do all of the following:
- Properly screen all personnel, including volunteers.
- Develop and implement policies for reporting and handling child sexual exploitation.
- Develop protocols for computer use to safeguard against Interest predators.
- Utilize age-appropriate safety programs.
- Make sure the physical structure of the school is safe and that children are always properly supervised.
- Provide interactive programs for parents—get the parents involved!

At the community level, responsible adults will take these steps:
- Develop community awareness of child sexual exploitation and the sex-offender registry.
- Support neighborhood watch group development.

- Support aggressive prosecution of offenders.
- Make the community child-safe.
- Ensure the presence of an abduction alert system, such as AMBER.
- Advocate use of Code Adam in local stores in response to a lost-child situation.
- Institute free child-identification programs.
- Advocate for legislative change as required.

AFTERWORD

Far too many American children grow up in unstable, potentially harmful environments. Many live in poverty, suffer malnutrition, have untended health problems, and live in unsafe homes. Many do not have a chance at a good education, training or enrichment. Many face the dangers of crime. Most children encounter the temptations and threats of drugs and alcohol, and all experience the blitz of music and media messages that undermine moral, responsible behavior. Few children are immune from modern pressures: 1 in 4 children lives with only one parent; between 16 and 33% are obese; about 25% of girls and 13% of boys have nonconsensual sex before age 18; teen suicides have tripled in the last three decades; and homicide is one of the leading killers or children with many killed by their own parents.

According to an article in the *Chicago Tribune*, the goals of a bipartisan National Commission on Children were: "Healthier, well-educated children; reduced public costs of health care and remedial education; decreased crime, violence and their associated costs; increased tax revenues and lower welfare payments; improved productivity of American industry and labor . . . stronger families; more active, inclusive communities; a freer, fairer society; a more optimistic citizenry." That was over 10 years ago. I guess we're still waiting.

The future of childhood starts now, and it begins with you. Let kids be kids.

REFERENCES

Print References

Andrews, S. (2004). US Domestic prosecution of the American International Sex Tourist: Efforts to protect children from sexual exploitation. *Journal of Criminal Law & Criminology, 94*(2), 415–454.

Araji, S. (1997). *Sexually Aggressive Children: Coming To Understand Them.* Thousand Oaks, CA: Sage Publications.

Ascione, F. (2001). Animal abuse and youth violence. *Office of Juvenile Justice and Delinquency Prevention Bulletin, NCJ 188677.* Retrieved March 15, 2003, from www.ncjrs.org/html/ojjdp/jjbul2001_9_2/contents.html

Barnitz, L. (2001). Effectively responding to the commercial sexual exploitation of children: A comprehensive approach to prevention, protection and reintegration. *Child Welfare, 80*(5), 597–611.

Becker, J., and Hunter, J. (1993). Aggressive sexual offenders. *Child and Adolescent Psychiatric Clinics of North America, 21,* 362–365.

Coles, R. (1990). *The Spiritual Life of Children.* Boston: Houghton Mifflin.

DeKlerk, V. (1991). Expletives: Men only? *Communications Monographs 58,* 156–196.

Deranek, T., and Gilman, D. (nd). Children as sex offenders, why? *ERIC.*

Edelman, C., and Mandle, C. (2002). *Health Promotion Throughout the Lifespan, 5th Edition.* St. Louis: CV Mosby.

(Editorial). (1991). Make children our first priority. *Chicago Tribune, June 30, p. 2.*

FBI. The cybersex offender and children.n (2005). *FBI Law Enforcement Bulletin, 74*(3), 12–17.

Finkelhor, D., and Ormrod, R. (2001). Child pornography: Patterns from NIBRS. *OJJDP Juvenile Justice Bulletin, December.*

Finkelhor, D., and Ormrod, R. (2004). Prostitution of children: Patterns from NIBRS. *OJJDP Juvenile Justice Bulletin, June.*

Fox, J. (2002). *Primary Health Care of Infants, Children & Adolescents, 2nd Edition.* St. Louis: CV Mosby.

Giroux, H. (2001). Stealing Innocence: Corporate Culture's War on Children. Palgrave MacMillian.

Honig, A. (2001). How to promote creative thinking. *Scholastic Early Childhood Today, 15*(5), 34–41.

Hunter, J. (2000). Understanding juvenile sex offenders: Research findings and guidelines for effective management and treatment. *Juvenile Forensic Evaluation Resource Center.* www.ilpp.virginia.edu/Publications_and_Reports.

Jalongo, M. (2003). The child's right to creative though and expression. *Childhood Education, 79*(4), 218–229.

Kim, W. (2001). What ever happened to play? *Time, 157*(17), 56–59.

Lanning, K. (2001). *Child molestors: A behavioral analysis, 4th Edition.* National Center for Missing and Exploited Children.

Leong, D., and Bodrova, E. (2003). An hour of play—what for? *Scholastic Early Childhood Today, 17*(5), 5.

Libby, T. (2005). Role models are essential for today's juniors to excel. *AKC Gazette, 122*(2), 18–19.

Lingren, H. (1996). Gangs: The new family. NebGuide. University of Nebraska. www.ianrpubs.unl.edu.

Mathews, R., Hunter, J., and Vuz, J. (1997). Juvenile female sexual offenders: clinical characteristics and treatment issues. *Sexual Abuse: Journal of Residential Treatment, 9,* 187–199.

Melson, G. (2003). Child development and the human-companion animal bond. *The American Behavioral Scientists, 47*(1), 31–35.

Mesnikoff, J. (2002). Practical responses to spiritual distress by nurse practitioners. *Clinical Excellence for Nurse Practitioners, 6*(3), 39.

Morgenthaler, S. (2001). Children and creativity. *Lutheran Education, 137*(1), 71–72.

Murray, R., and Zentner, J. (2001). *Health Promotion Strategies Through the Lifespan, 7th Edition.* Upper Saddle River, NJ: Prentice Hall.

Muscari, M. (2004). *Not My Kid 2: Protecting Your Children from the 21 Threats of the 21st Century.* Scranton, PA: University of Scranton Press.

Muscari, M. (2002). *Not My Kid: 21 Steps to Raising a Nonviolent Child.* Scranton, PA: University of Scranton Press.

National Association of Early Childhood Specialists in the State Department of Education. (2000). Recess and the importance of play: A position statement on young children and recess.

Norvilitis, J., and Santa Maria, P. (2002). Credit card debt on college campuses: Causes, consequences, and solutions. *College Student Journal, 36*(3), 356–364.

Packer, J., and Quisenberry, N. (2002). Play: Essential for all children. *Childhood Education, 79*(1), 33–40.

Perina, K. (2004). Where have all the idols gone. *Psychology Today, 37*(4), 3.

Presbury, J., and Benson, A. (1990). Children and creativity. National Association of School Psychologists.

Quinn, K. (2000). Animal abuse at early age linked to interpersonal violence. *The Brown University Child and Adolescent Behavior Letter, 16*(3), 1–3.

Riebel, L. (2005). Psychology and consumer culture: The struggle for a good life in a materialistic world. *Psychotherapy: Theory, Research, Practice, Training, 42*(1), 122–123.

Roberts, J., and Jones, E. (2001). Money attitudes, credit card use, and compulsive buying among Amerian college students. *The Journal of Consumer Affairs, 35*(2), 213–241.

Santrock, J. (2003). *Children, 7th Edition.* Madison, WI: Brown & Benchmark.

Stevens, S. (2003). Creative expressions in free play. *Music Educators Journal, 89*(5), 44–47.

Taylor, A., Kuo, F., and Sullivan. (2001). Coping with ADD: The surprising connection to green play settings. *Environment and Beahvior, 33*(1), 54–77.

Toruati, J., and Barber, J. (2005). Dancing with trees: Infants and toddlers in the garden. *YC Young Children, 60*(3), 40–47.

Wells, N., and Evans, G. (2003). A buffer of life stress among rural children. *Environment and Behavior, 35*(3), 311–330.

Wells, N., and Evans, G. (2000). At home with nature: Effects of "greenness" on children's cognitive functioning. *Environment and Behavior, 32*(6), 775–795.

Woodside, C. (2002). Bring back recess. *The Washington Post.* December 8, 2002. p B7.

Zavitkovsky, D. (2001). On creativity and young children. *Scholastic Early Childhood, 15*(5), 41.

Web References

_____(nd). Celebrating uniqueness. Positive Parenting. www.wordsofdiscovery.com.

_____(2005). Citizenship. American Family Traditions. www.americanfamilytraditions.com.

_____. (nd). Creativity and play. www.pbs.org.

_____. (2001). Debt Nation. www.pbs.org.

_____. (nd). Down and dirty family fun. www.homebasics.com.

_____. (1999). Families first – keys to successful family function: roles. Virginia State University Cooperative Extension. http://www.ext.vt.edu/pubs/family/350–093/350–093.html.

_____. (2004). Got obnoxious offspring? It could be your fault! www.msnbc.com.

_____(nd). Heroes in every community. Texas Extension Education Association: Texas Cooperative Extension. www.tamu.edu.

_____(2004). Parenting: Attachment, bonding and reactive attachment disorder. www.helpguide.org.

Abel, K. (nd). From Spiderman to mom: How kids choose heroes. www.familyeducation.com.

Anderson, K. (2002). Parents or pop culture? Children's heroes and role models. Association for Childhood Education International. www.findarticles.com.

Ashbridge, A. (2005). Cemeteries still recovering from '04 vandalism. The Daily Star. www.dailystar.com.

Barhyte, D. (nd). Simply grand: The importance of grandparents. Grandparents Today. www.grandparentstoday.com.

Barron, T. (2004). Teaching the difference between celebrities and heroes. Chicogo Parent. www.tabarron.com.

Bartel, M. (2001). Nine classroom creativity killers. www.goshen.edu.

Bradway, L. (nd). Cornucopia Kids: Children who have too much stuff. Main Street Mom. www.mainstreetmom.com.

Bush, V. (2004). The great outdoors: want a simple way to bond with your kids? Head outdoors! *Essence.* www.findarticles.com.

Campbell, E. (2004). After Sept. 11: Heroes in a post-Sept. 11 world. Susquehanna Valley Parent Magazine. www.svparent.com.

Clements, R. (2005). Play in the dirt for a clean bill of health. www.newsforparents.com.

Cromie, W. The whys and woes of beauty pageants. *The Harvard University Gazette.* www.news.harvard.edu/gazette.

Darling, N. (1999). Parenting style and its correlates. www.athealth.com.

Denenberg, D. (nd). Yes, Harold, there are heroes! www.muweb.millersville.edu.

Donaldson, R. (2001). Role of parents and heroes. www.brainsarefun.com.

Elkind, D. (2003). The Overbooked Child. *Psychology Today, Jan-Feb.* www.psychologytoday.com.

Foster, H. (nd). Nurturing Children's Spirituality. www.familiesonline.co.uk.

Foston, N. (2004). Teaching spirituality: give your childen a lesson they can follow all year. *Ebony.* www.findarticles.com.

Frank, B. (nd) Boredom. Homeschool in the LINK. www.homeschoolnewslink.com

Frank, C., and Hester, S. 603/607 Thematic Unit/Good Citizenship. www.unr.edu.

Gardner, M. (2005). For all who have never climbed a tree. *The Christian Science Monitor, May 25.* www.csmonitor.com.

Gibbons, W. (nd). How do you reconnect kids to nature? University of Georgia. www.uga.edu.

Gibbs, N. (2001). Do kids have too much power? www.Time.com.

Gibson, E. (nd). The need for play. www.elainegibson.net.

Goleman, D., and Kaufman, P. (1992). The art of creativity. *Psychology Today, March.*

Hanser, M. (2005). Healing the spiritual dimension: A Christian perspective. National Center of Coninuing Education. www.nursece.com.

Klein, H. (1998). One of a kind: Individuality in children. Association for Childhood Education. www.findarticles.com.

Johnson, D. (2002). Five things to do outdoors with children. www.earlychildhood.com.

Lawton, W. (2005). Raising heroes. Focus on the Family. www.family.org.

Lopes, M. (1995). Creative play helps children grow. National Network for Child Care. www.nncc.org.

MacPherson, K. (2002). Creative play makes better problem solvers. Pittsburgh Post-Gazette. www.post-gazette.com.

MacPherson, K. (2002). Development experts say children suffer due to lack of unstructured fun. Pittsburgh Post-Gazette. www.post-gazette.com.

MacPherson, K. (2002). Experts call unstructured play essential to children's growth. Pittsburgh Post-Gazette. www.post-gazette.com.

Milloy, M. (2002). Girls, interrupted: the terrible world of child prostitution—the war on girls. Essence Communications. www.findarticles.com.

Minderovic, Z. (1998). Spirituality in children. Gale Encyclopedia of Childhood and Adolescence. www.findarticles.com.

Mindock, P. (nd). Kids dig dirt: Gardening with your children. Great Lakes Families. www.cribnotes.com.

Moran, J. (2004). Creativity in Young Children. www.kidssource.com.

Nussbaum, K. Children and Beauty Pageants. *A Minor Consideration.* www.minorcon.org.

O'Connell, T. (1999). Give your children heroes. www.timoconnell.com.

Perry, B. (nd). Attachment: The first core strength. Teachers Scholastic. www.teacher_scholastic.com.

Pica, R. (2002). Take it outside! www.earlychildhood.com.

Ponton, L. (2004). Sexual abuse of boys by clergy. Adolescent Psychiatry. www.findarticles.com.

Powell, E. (2005). Many teens carrying credit, debt cards—and carrying balances. The Pittsburgh Post-Gazette. www.post-gazette.com.

Ransford, M. Professor says beauty pageants aren't for kids. *Newscenter.* www.bsu.edu/news/article.

Riley, D. (1996). Helping to form a secure attachment. National Network for Child Care. www.nncc.org.

Schaffer, S. (2005). Fighting gangs in Scranton. 16WNEP The News Station. www.wnep.com.

Sohn, E. (2004). Nature may nurture paying attention. www.sciencenewsforkids.com.

Spun, B. (2002). Closed doors and childhoods lost. News World Communications. www.findarticles.com

Swartz, J. Schoolyard bullies get nastier online: www.USAToday.com.

Thomas, J. (nd). Materialistic parents, materialistic children. www.preventdisease.com.

US Surgeon General. (2005). US Surgeon General gives tips to fathers and fathers-to-be: Father's Day tips for a healthy childhood. http://www.surgeongeneral.gov/pressreleases/sg06172005.html

White, R. (nd). Interaction with nature during the middle years: Its importance in children's development & nature's future. www.whitehutchinson.com.

Wilson, L. (2002). On killing creativity in children. www.pwsp.edu.

Wiser, B. (nd). Nature-deficit disorder and what you can do about it. www.bruderhof.com.

Yin, S. (2004). A rude awakening. *American Demographics.* www.findarticles.com.

About: www.about.com

About Kids: www.aboutkidshealth.com

American Academy of Pediatrics: www.aap.org

American Association for the Child's Right to Play: www.piausa.org

Ask Dr. Sears: www.askdrsears.com

Crime Library: www.crimelibrary.com

Cyberbullying: www.cyberbully.org

KidsHealth: www.kidshealth.org

Kids Source: www.kidsource.com

Merriam-Webster Online: www.m-w.com

My Hero: www.myhero.com

National Center for Missing and Exploited Children: www.ncmec.org

National Youth Violence Prevention Resource Center: www.safeyouth.org

Parenthood: www.parenthood.com

Protect Kids: www.protectkids.com

Psychology Foundation of Canada: www.psychologyfoundation.org

Spook Shows: www.spookshows.com (information on King Zor)

Teenagers Today: www.teenagerstoday.com

US Department of Justice: www.usdoj.gov

Whole Family: www.wholefamily.com